l.c. 3/16

D0899751

# Take a Bow!

Lesson Plans for Preschool Drama

# Smith and Kraus
# Instructional Books for Teachers Series

Johnson, Maureen Brady. *Middle Mania! Imaginative Theater Projects for Middle School Actors.*

———. *Middle Mania Two! Imaginative Theater Projects for Middle School Actors.*

Landalf, Helen. *Moving the Earth: Teaching Earth Science Through Movement, Grades 3–6.*

———. *Moving Is Relating: Developing Interpersonal Skills Through Movement, Grades 3–6.*

Landalf, Helen, and Pamela Gerke. *Drama Curriculum for Grades K–1: Hooves and Horns, Fins and Feathers*

———. *Drama Curriculum for Grades 2–3: Mail and Mystery, Family and Friends.*

———. *Movement Stories for Children, Ages 3–6.*

McCullough, L. E. *Anyone Can Produce Plays with Kids!*

Ostler, Fredi, and Rick Hamilton. *Macbeth: A Workbook for Students.*

———. *A Midsummer Night's Dream: A Workbook for Students.*

———. *Much Ado About Nothing: A Workbook for Students.*

———. *Romeo and Juliet: A Workbook for Students.*

———. *The Taming of the Shrew: A Workbook for Students.*

Thistle, Louise. *Aesop's Fables.*

———. *Classic Poetry for Middle and High School Students.*

———. *Greek Mythology.*

———. *Mother Goose.*

———. *Myths and Tales.*

———. *Three Classic Tales.*

———. *Dramatizando Tres Cuentos Clasicos.*

Varley, Joy. *Places, Please! A Manual for High School Theater Directors.*

If you require prepublication information about upcoming Smith and Kraus books, you may receive our catalogue, free of charge, by sending your name and address to Smith and Kraus Catalogue, PO Box 127, Lyme, NH 03768. Or call us at (800) 895-4331.

# Take a Bow!

## Lesson Plans for Preschool Drama

By Nina Czitrom

YOUNG ACTORS SERIES

A Smith and Kraus Book

Published by Smith and Kraus, Inc.
177 Lyme Road, Hanover, NH 03755
www.smithkraus.com

First Edition: April 2004
Manufactured in the United States of America
10 9 8 7 6 5 4 3 2 1

*Cover and text design by Julia Gignoux, Freedom Hill Design*

Library of Congress Cataloging-in-Publication Data
Czitrom, Nina.
Take a bow! : lesson plans for preschool drama / by Nina Czitrom. —1st ed.
P. cm. — (Young actors series)
ISBN 1-57525-341-0
1. Drama in education—study and teaching (Preschool) I. Title. II. Young actors series.

PN3171.C93 2003
372.66'044—d22
2003068619

# Special Thanks

With special thanks to Jacqueline Marks at the Children's International Workshop for giving me full license to find my way in creating drama lessons that have shaped my work, to Kia Woods of the Children's Garden Studio for her help with the photographs and her support, to George and Janet Chen for access to the beautiful pictures, to Daniel Czitrom for his support and invaluable guidance in this process, to my parents for their encouragement, and to David for believing in the idea and helping me to follow through all the way to the end.

# Contents

# UNIT 1
# The Basics

# Why Drama?

If you are new to the preschool age group, you may wonder why children this young will benefit from drama. And, if you're experienced with the preschoolers, perhaps you wonder how a drama class can be successful with such a young group. The how will be explained in detail throughout this book. The why is simple.

Every day preschool students wake up and watch their favorite television shows and become enraptured in thoughts of being the characters from these programs. They go to school and act out stories from these shows with their friends. They live inside the land of make-believe for a greater portion of their day because children ages three through five have the most creative and active imaginations of any age group. In this book, we use this capability as a natural learning tool and as a way to grow.

The lesson plans in this book are divided into four sections, each geared toward a different facet of the preschool child's mind. In Unit 3: Stories and Fairy Tales, children will begin to gain confidence by standing in front of their peers and becoming a part of the story. The Adventure Stories in Unit 4 will expand their minds and help them imagine new places while encouraging cooperation and a sense of togetherness. As we learn the Moral Lessons form the units, students will engage in storytelling to learn right from wrong in a variety of different settings and through numerous circumstances. Finally, Unit 6: New Ideas will introduce students to new words and concepts in a way that makes these things fit their concept of reality.

Drama is a wonderful aid in building the preschool child's attention span. Some children may not have the stamina to make it through an entire lesson when you first begin to teach drama. At this age, they are just learning how to sit for extended periods of time and how to listen carefully to directions. But as your students attend drama regularly, you will notice that the child who initially could not sit still will be wide-eyed and attentive for longer periods of time after just a few weeks. It's just another way they learn and grow through drama.

# Organizing and Executing Your Drama Lesson

## DRAMA AS STORYTELLING

In the simplest terms, drama is storytelling. It's the best way for actors to remember their job on stage, and it's the best way for you to explain to your students what they will be doing in drama class: They will be telling stories. The easiest way to explain what they will be acting out each day is by introducing your lesson as "the story of." In addition, this explanation will ensure that your students understand that drama class isn't about them playing the lead. It's a place where the whole class helps to tell a story.

# CLASS SIZE

For the preschool age group, the optimum number of children to have in your drama class is approximately eight. The lessons in this book can and will work with any number of students, ranging from five to twenty children. However, to give each student a chance to thrive and find his or her voice through these lessons, it's best to keep the class size down to ten children. If you attempt larger class sizes, you may find that students' relationships with others will begin to dominate class dynamics, and competition for attention will rule their actions.

# WATCHING SPACE AND PERFORMING SPACE

No matter what kind of space you have to teach your drama class, you should create two separate areas: a performing space and a watching space. These two spaces should remain consistent. The best way to create this stage/audience effect is with chairs.

Watching Space. The watching space should be one single row of chairs. This is where your students sit when their characters are not in the immediate telling of the story. You want them to be able to get in and out of their seats easily. They will watch and listen to the story from the watching space and will wait eagerly in these seats for the time when their parts come. It's best if the chairs are set up against a wall so that your performing space can be as large as possible.

Performing Space. If your classroom is a wide-open space without clearly defined borders, you will need to explain to your students where the borders of the performing space are by, for example, standing on the edge of that space. You may need to do this for the first few lessons to make it clear to them that they are to stay within the prescribed performing area. But they will quickly learn, and it will soon become a standard part of drama to them.

# THE THREE SECTIONS OF YOUR LESSON

It will be helpful to break your drama lesson into three sections: the warm-up, the story, and your follow-up activities. Using this format, the average drama lesson will last approximately forty-five minutes, with fifteen minutes for each section.

Warm-up. The warm-up (specific exercises explained in Unit 2) is designed to redirect the children's attention from the distractions of their preschool day and focus it on the drama class. As they begin to warm up, the children will start to imagine things. Their attention will turn from their toys and recent activities to the performing space. During your warm-up, you may find that the students who are often hesitant to get involved in other school activities will have the courage to become a part of drama class.

Story. The story will usually be the main focus of your drama lesson, especially for your eager students who have been waiting to find out what story they will be telling today. It's helpful to clearly define the beginning and ending of your story (usually the tags "once upon a time" and "the end" will be sufficient to accomplish this). You will be the narrator of this story, and you will call up each student to the performing space as his or her part comes up. In this book, each lesson will provide you with a synopsis of the story followed by a section titled Narrator, designed to guide you through the telling of the story with your students. There's no need to memorize these stories. As long as you know the basic story, you're set and ready to go.

Follow-ups. The follow-ups are additional activities that are designed to apply the story to the student's everyday life. In this book, you will usually find three kinds of follow-ups: (1) a learning lesson, (2) a follow-up that is just for fun and expanding the imagination, and (3) a confidence builder. It's often a good idea to draw on a couple of these activities so as to keep your lesson fun as well as educational.

## KEEPING IT SAFE

It's important to explain to your students that everything done in drama is pretend. You may have to remind them of this during every lesson. A good story revolves around conflict, and sometimes the children will become involved in the conflict that has been created in the performing space. They may get caught up in the story, thinking it's OK to grab another child. When you gently remind them that the story is pretend, they will remember where they are, what rules apply in school, and scale their behavior back accordingly.

# Assigning Roles

## CHOOSING A CHARACTER

Children act out their fears and realize their dreams through role play. It's an important part of their emotional growth. So, it's essential to let each child choose the character that he or she would like to play. When you list off the characters who appear in the story that you are about to tell, you will find that each child usually identifies with one specific role. Let him or her play that part in the story. You'll find that some students will always want to play the mother character, and others may always want to be the bad guy. This kind of repetition is fine. It usually means that there is something about that particular persona that the student needs to work out, and drama is the right place to do it.

## CAN *HE* BE CINDERELLA? CAN *SHE* BE THE KING?

There will be some students who pay no attention to the gender of a role. This is fine. You should encourage your students to play any role they want, even if a boy wants to play a girl or a girl wants to play a boy. Drama is not a place for stereotyping or limiting a child's imagination. It's a place where children can explore and develop new parts of themselves. Again, there may just be something about that role that speaks to the student. There may also be someone like that character missing from the child's life, especially if the role is a mother or a father. Remember to keep an open mind and to let your students find what's right for them.

## HOW MANY BIG BAD WOLVES CAN I HAVE ANYWAY?

There will rarely be enough roles for each child to have one all to him- or herself, and it will be even more rare that the parts get spread out evenly. Most times you will have to double, triple, even quadruple up on a few of the roles. This is absolutely acceptable. In fact, it will often help the student who is too shy either to say the lines or to get up in front of the class by him- or herself. The more the merrier. Just remember, there's no need for each child to say the character's lines separately from the others. All five of your Big Bad Wolves can tell the Little Pigs to let them in at the same time. There's strength in numbers. Finally, you will play whatever roles have not been filled by the student's requests, which usually makes your job more fun.

## YOUR ROLE AS THE NARRATOR

You get to play a part in this story too. Your role is the Narrator. You will be the one telling the most essential parts of the story: giving exposition, describing the setting, and telling the children where they come in during the tale. This includes telling them what to say when it's their turn. When it's time for a student to say a line, there is no need to whisper it in his or her ear first. As the Narrator, you can narrate what a character says, and your students repeat their lines after you. For example, when you say, "Goldilocks ate the first bowl of porridge and said, "Yuck, too hot!," the student who is playing Goldilocks immediately knows that she is supposed to say, "Yuck, too hot!" and responds accordingly. Children are attentive to stories. You'll be amazed at how quickly they catch on. In the lesson plans described in this book, the stories are written out for your convenience. Feel free to add or delete any parts from them that you feel may be too cumbersome for your students to handle. Just remember to keep your narration light and exciting.

# Separating the Story from the Classroom

It's important to keep the story that you tell in drama class separate from the everyday playing that occurs in your preschool or learning center. Always make clear to your students that the character they are playing and the circumstances of the story are only to be played out in drama class. Otherwise, a child faces the danger of walking around all day continuing to be Snow

White instead of facing the reality of the school setting. It's not easy for a child to learn her ABCs while focusing on her friends, the Dwarfs.

For this reason, it's always a good idea to stress the beginning and ending of your story in a clear way. A great way to do this is by starting your story with the phrase "once upon a time" and always ending with "the end." If you keep this consistent, your students will have no trouble deciphering when they are in the world of the story and when they are not.

Some additional ways to help them shed a character's skin may be necessary. In a child's mind, the end of a story has no bearing on the life of a character. Listed below are some methods for getting your students to separate themselves from the story at its conclusion. Choose the one that you think would be the most fun for you and your students.

- Direct your students to an imaginary car (complete with seat belts, ignition key, and buttons to press for fun) and drive away from the story, saying good-bye to all the different characters as you leave. You may be driving back to school together, or you may be driving to another make-believe place where you will conduct your follow-up activities. Choose what's most fun for you.

- After the students take their bow at the end of the story, literally have them pretend to take off their character suit from top to bottom. Once they slip out of it, they can say good-bye to that persona for the rest of the day.

- Open up an imaginary door and let each child walk out of the land of make-believe. As they say good-bye to the role they played, the students can explain to the character that they have to go back to school now. It's a good way to keep the pretending going for a moment longer.

## TAKING A BOW

At the end of each story, you should always have your students stand up together and take a big giant bow. Not only will this further define the ending of your story, but it will also serve as a little reward to your students for participating in the story and for having the courage to make it all the way through to the end.

# UNIT 2
# Warm-ups

# How Are You Feeling?

## OBJECTIVES

- To continually educate students about what a feeling is and how to identify a feeling within themselves

- For the teacher to gauge the emotional states of the students on a particular day (one of the students may still be fuming over the fact that he or she didn't get to press the button in the elevator this morning, while another may be sad that his or her mother just left to go to work)

- To have the students acknowledge these feelings before beginning class so that the feelings do not manifest during the lesson or throughout the remainder of the day.

## ACTIVITIES

**The Circle of Feelings.** Begin by sitting in a circle with your students. Go around the circle and ask each child how he or she is feeling today. When the student gives you an answer, ask him why he is feeling this way. No matter how your students are feeling, it's important to give them positive reinforcement regarding what they have just shared with you and the rest of the class. Whether someone is happy today because he has a new shirt on or another child is angry because she didn't get to sit next to her friend when she sat down, it's important for each student to know that how he or she is feeling in this moment is OK. For help on teaching your students about feelings, see "The Feeling Story" in Unit 6.

**Faces.** Practice making the faces that each feeling evokes. Ask your students to make a happy face or a sad face and see what their experience is like. They may not know what certain feelings are, so you may need to add a description. By making the face with them, they will learn the basic idea of a feeling from your example. Some faces to try might be:

| | | |
|---|---|---|
| Happy | Shy | Confused |
| Sad | Embarrassed | Scared |
| Angry | Tired | Scary |
| Jealous | Excited | Silly |

Once you've tried a face, be sure to have the students erase it with imaginary eraser-hands. This will help to ensure that you are starting with a clean slate on each emotion and will wipe away the final face so you can be certain of ending with neutrality. After all, you don't want them to walk around with their scary faces on for the next hour.

# Shakin' It Out

## OBJECTIVES

- To warm up the body
- To let go of any existing inhibitions

## ACTIVITIES

**The Shakes.** While standing with your students, have them shake out their arms in different directions. To make it a little more fun and silly, incorporate a sound with each movement. Some ways to shake it out are:

Arms above your head

Arms down to the ground

Out to the sides

To the right and then left side

Behind you

Over your head as you turn around in a circle

Over your head as your shake your whole body

**The Wiggles.** Have your students get a case of "the wiggles" in various body parts. Try to see if they can isolate a particular body part as they wiggle and wriggle it. Good parts to wiggle are:

| | | |
|---|---|---|
| Fingers | Nose | Belly button |
| Wrists | Eyebrows | Hips |
| Elbows | Hair | Knees |
| Shoulders | Ears | Toes |
| Chin | Lips | |

**Count Down.** Tell your students that they are going to shake their arms and legs a specific number of times. Start by having them shake their right arms over their heads five times, then their left arms, followed by their right legs five times, and then their left legs. When they've finished, start over again with the next number down, shaking each arm and leg four times. The real fun begins when you get down to the number 1. Watch out for those flailing arms and legs as your students get downright silly.

# Remember Who Your Friends Are

## OBJECTIVES

- To encourage interaction among students
- To introduce the concept of working together

## ACTIVITIES

Freeze. Have your students casually walk around the performing space as a group. At random moments call out for them to freeze. Encourage them to stop moving as soon as they hear the word *freeze*. This activity, though unbelievably simple, is great for reflex development and listening skills.

High-Fives. After your students have gotten used to the idea of freezing at your direction, it's time to add some fun to it. Continue walking around the performing space with your students, but this time when they hear the word *freeze* they are going to go up to someone and give them a high-five. Do this variation a few times and encourage them to find a different student for each turn.

Handshakes. This is the same concept as the high-fives, but this time when you say freeze, students will go up to someone and shake his or her hand.

Introduce Yourself. This time when you say freeze, have your students find one person and tell him or her their name. Undoubtedly, your students already know each other's names, but that is not what this activity is really about: It's to help your students take charge and interact with one another.

Colors. This time when you say freeze, your students will tell another student what his or her favorite color is. Here are some other "freeze" variations:

- Tell someone your favorite animal.
- Tell someone your favorite food.
- Tell someone how old you are.
- Name a color of something you're wearing.
- Make a funny shape with your fingers.
- Make a shape with your arms.
- Make a shape with your legs.

# The Walks of Life

## OBJECTIVES

- To get students to respond quickly to direction
- To improve the students' ability to think on their feet
- To continue and encourage the students to work as a group
- To begin the journey into the world of make-believe

## ACTIVITIES

**Slow Walk.** Have your students walk around the performing space as slowly as possible. Encourage them to move their entire body — arms, hands, faces — at this slow pace. Once they have the hang of this and have experimented with it for a minute or two, have the children go up to someone and shake hands with him or her as slowly as possible. This is great as a calming exercise, especially for children with lots of energy.

**Fast Walk.** Direct the students to walk around the room as quickly as they can. It's always helpful to remind them to walk fast rather than run, since they already know how to run. The real challenge here is to walk with a quickened pace.

**Mouse Steps.** Have your students continue walking around the space, this time with teeny-tiny steps. It may help to compare this movement with little mouse steps. Once they have their steps as small as possible, encourage them to run like a mouse, with itty-bitty steps.

**Elephant Steps.** Now your students will take the biggest, most gigantic steps that they possibly can. You can compare it to a variety of enormous animals, but elephants are less aggressive and will therefore cause the least amount of distraction during the activity. Encourage your students to not only move their legs with big steps, but their arms, too.

**March.** A marching step is always a fun one for the children. Suggest that they choose an instrument to play and make a pretend marching band.

**Sideways.** Direct your students to walk sideways. It helps them to get the idea if you participate in this one as well. Once they can walk sideways, have them skip sideways. To mix it up a little more, have them freeze and then change directions. Repeat this last part as many times as you want. Instead of tiring of the exercise, they will gain energy and excitement. It's also a great way to increase listening skills and reflex control.

Backward. If you trust your students enough to know that they won't get out of control with this one, have them walk backward. Most likely, they will be apprehensive enough about it that they will not start running backward. It's always fun to add sounds with this one. For instance, a "whoa" or a "boink" will always add some silliness to the activity.

Skipping. Have your students skip around the space together (all in the same direction works best). You can add to this activity by singing "Skip to My Lou" as the students round the room. After each verse, try singing it a little faster. As you get faster, remind your students that they can skip faster with the music, but they must skip and not run. It's more challenging for your students and keeps the activity safe.

Hot Sand. Now tell the children to walk around the room as though they were walking on hot, hot sand. They will want to lift their feet off the floor as quickly as they can because the sand will burn their feet. It adds to the fun to include an "ooch" or an "ouch" to the activity to give them the idea.

Trampolines. It's time to bounce on trampolines. Encourage your students to bounce around the whole room on their trampolines. Have them bounce off for a rest occasionally, and then have them bounce back on. You can help them wrap their mind around this one by accompanying the activity with "boing, boing" as though you were making the sound of springs.

Airplanes. Then it's time to fly around the room like airplanes. Have your students grow wings and take flight throughout the performing space. After a while, you may want to have them all come in for a landing. Once they're all seated on the floor in their landing positions, remind them that only one airplane at a time can take off from an airport. You will clear each child for take-off by calling his or her name. Once their name has been called, they are free to fly around the room again and to explore the skies.

# Animals

## OBJECTIVES

- To move fully into the realm of make-believe
- To encourage interaction among students

## ACTIVITIES

There activities involve exploring different animals. You will ask the group, as a whole, to become creature after creature, complete with sounds and movements. You can choose as many or as few as you like to experiment with during each lesson. As they become these creatures, give them a minute or two to explore each animal and try to encourage interaction between the students. Foremost, you'll want to focus the students on the idea of simply becoming these animals. Included in this section are a number of ideas and variations to add to the activity once your students have grasped each animal.

Birds. Have your students fly around the room like birds. Remember that some birds have tiny wings and others have large ones. Leave the decision up to your students as to which sort of bird they will be. You can also have your students land on a branch for a moment or two, or have them build a little nest.

Cats. Have your students crawl around the room as kitties while talking to the other cats. They can communicate through meows. You can remind your students that the way a cat gets clean is by licking itself. Encourage your students to take a pretend cat bath. Explore the different sounds that cats make. Sometimes they meow, other times they purr. As they interact, have the children experiment with these sounds.

Dogs. Your students will happily crawl around the performing space like dogs. Be sure to explore how dogs wag their tails when they are happy, how they bark when they want something, and how they love to run around and play. Have the dogs dig a hole in the ground and bury a bone or a toy, then return to the burial place and dig it up again. Practice some dog tricks like sitting and rolling over.

Elephants. Elephants take big steps. When they walk, their big trunks swing from side to side. Have your students use their arms as trunks and stomp around the room making elephant calls. Encourage your students to use their elephant trunks; sometimes they can be used to drink water or to give themselves a bath. One arm can be being used as a trunk and the other as a tail. Have the elephants link up, trunks to tails, and continue stomping around the space.

**Turtles.** The turtles can explore the many uses of their turtle shells. The turtles can walk around when all of a sudden, something comes and scares them — and they hide in their shells. They can peek out when they think it's safe. Repeat this a few times: The children will get a kick out of hiding from you. When it's time for the turtles to go to sleep, they can retreat into their shells again so that nothing can harm them while they're resting.

**Monkeys.** Monkeys make interesting and silly noises and are high-energy animals. Make sure that your students communicate with one another using their monkey sounds. It's always fun to have the monkeys climb up a tree and swing from tree to tree on some vines. This activity can be accompanied by many different sounds. Monkeys always like to take a banana break. Have your monkeys peel and eat some bananas. Perhaps they can share with one another.

**Dolphins.** As your students swim around the room like dolphins, every now and then have them jump out of the water and then swim deep into the ocean again. This can be repeated several times, as it's always fun to jump. The dolphins can also communicate with one another. Ask your students what sound they think a dolphin makes. It's better to go with their perception of the sound than to make one up that they cannot identify. The students can also open their mouths wide and eat some fish that are floating around.

**Penguins.** Penguins have a funny walk, which can be acted out by having your students walk on their heels with their arms at their sides. From time to time, have the penguins dive into the icy water and take a swim.

**Pigs.** Have your students crawl around and make oinking sounds as they become pigs. Your students will enjoy learning that pigs love to roll around in the mud. Have the children roll around in their pretend sty and get all muddy. Make sure to hose them off if they come over to get mud on you.

**Giraffes.** It can be difficult to act out this animal. Have your students try to make their necks as long as they can while trying to become a giraffe. You may want to have them eat leaves off trees like giraffes. They will have to stretch their necks even more to reach them, but they will enjoy the effort. Have your giraffes get excited and gallop around the room. This can be done on all fours or in a standing position.

**Skunks.** Skunks can walk around like cats do, except with one added feature. As your skunks are walking around the room, pretend that you are scaring them with a noise. This should send their tails in the air as they spray out a stinky aroma. Have them smell it afterward. Usually, a little "pee-you" will help add some comedy to this activity.

Snakes. The snakes can slither around the room as they hiss at one another in a friendly way. Have the snakes go to sleep. As they do this, they will need to coil themselves up into circles. It's physically difficult for a child to do this, but it's worth the try so they can really delve into the life of this creature. Snakes often shed their skins. Your students can shed their skins by slowly wriggling out of them. Once they've done that, the snake may feel re-freshed and may want to slither around some more.

Frogs. It's always fun for students to hop around the room and "ribbit" while becoming a frog. The frogs can jump from lily pad to lily pad in a little game of tag with one another. Have them communicate through their frog sounds as they play this game. Frogs eat by sticking out their long, sticky tongues and grabbing up insects. Have your frogs do this as they try to catch some flies.

Bumblebees. The students will flap their wings and buzz around as they fly through the space as bumble bees. The bees can stop at their beehive to make some honey with the rest of the bees. This is both a great group activity and something that really promotes cooper-ation. When bumblebees get scared, they sting. Have your students pretend to be scared from a noise or a sound that you make and sting an imaginary person. But the bumblebees die once they do this. Your students will enjoy dropping to the ground as dead bees. It sounds morbid, but children find it interesting and funny.

Caterpillar/Butterfly. Your students can crawl, slither, or inch around the room as little caterpillars. They may want to stop and eat a few leaves, as caterpillars often do. Once they've spent some time as caterpillars, it's time to change into beautiful butterflies. Have them stretch their wings for the first time and begin to fly around the room with one an-other. You many want to ask each butterfly to tell the class what color he or she is.

Little Boys and Girls. In the last activity, have your students turn back into little boys and girls. The students will simply walk around the room as they normally would. They obviously know how to do this, but it will help to close the activity in a neutral state be-fore moving on to your story.

# UNIT 3
## Stories and Fairy Tales

In this unit, your students will begin to gain confidence by standing in front of their peers and acting out familiar stories. Your students have heard or read most of the stories and fairy tales used in this unit, so they may feel more comfortable beginning with these stories. The characters may be like old friends to them.

Keep in mind how well children remember the details of their favorite tales. You will find that if your students know any of these stories by heart, the slightest change will cause them to stop the narration and tell you how it really goes, especially if they've got it on video at home. Therefore, you may want to preface your storytelling by explaining to the students that they will be working on the drama version of the story. Encourage them to explore the uniqueness of this version. It will add a sense of play for them.

For your convenience, the stories at the beginning of this unit are simple and increase in difficulty as the unit continues. However, don't be scared by the more "difficult" ones. They simply have more characters and slightly more complicated plot lines. But, they're still fairy tales!

# The Three Little Pigs

## OBJECTIVES

- To engage students through storytelling
- To encourage students to work together
- To teach students about being nice to others

## ROLES FOR STUDENTS TO CHOOSE FROM

| Role | Selling Point for the Students |
|---|---|
| The Pigs | Gets to build and create |
| The Big Bad Wolf | Gets to be the bad guy |

You can have as many pigs and as many wolves as you wish. You don't have to limit your number of pigs just because the story is called "The Three Little Pigs."

## STORY SYNOPSIS

Once upon a time there were three Pigs who wanted to build a house. First, they built one out of straw. But the Big Bad Wolf, who wanted to eat the Pigs, came along and blew it down. Next, the Pigs built a house out of sticks. But again, the Wolf came and blew it down. Finally, the Pigs built the strongest house of all out of bricks. This time, no matter how hard he tried, the Wolf couldn't blow the house in. So he tried to get in through the chimney. When he slid down to the fireplace, he burned his bottom, ran out the front door, and never bothered the Pigs again. The Pigs did not get eaten by the Wolf. They lived in their brick house happily ever after.

## NARRATOR

Once upon a time there were three Pigs that loved to play together. One day, _____ said, "I have an idea. Let's build a house out of straw!" The other Pigs thought this was a great idea. So they began to build. When they were done, they sat down inside their house of straw.

> *Have the students who are playing the Pigs come to the performing space to play together. When the student, whose name you have inserted, hears what he or she is supposed to say, he or she will repeat it after you. Have the Pigs begin to build that house out of straw. Then, upon your narration, have the Pigs sit down all together inside this house.*

They were just sitting down to dinner when, all of a sudden, along came a Big Bad Wolf. He was very hungry. He had seen the Pigs building all day, and he wanted to eat them for dinner.

> *When they hear you talk about dinner, the Pigs will pretend to eat a big meal. Have them stuff their faces as ravenously as you like. They'll enjoy making a pretend mess. As you introduce the Big Bad Wolf, have your Wolf, or Wolves, enter the performing space. They can make their hungry faces and even lick their lips if you like. It helps if you do this with them so they'll get the hang of it.*

He knocked on the door, and the Pigs said, "Who is it?" The Wolf replied, "Little pigs, little pigs, let me in." And the Pigs said, "Not by the hair on our chinny chin chins." The Wolf said, "Then I'll huff, and I'll puff, and I'll blow your house in," and he did.

> *Encourage the Wolves to knock on the door as you narrate the knocking. It's perfectly fine for you to do these activities as well, so that the students may follow your example. As you narrate this dialogue, your students can repeat it after you. Make sure to break it up into small sections, sentence by sentence, so that it won't be too much for them to remember. They'll know when their part comes when you narrate whether the Pigs or the Wolves speak. When it comes time for the Wolves to blow down the house, have the Wolves blow as hard as they can.*

The house fell down, and the Pigs began to run. The Wolf tried to catch them, but he could not.

> *Children love nothing more than a big chase scene. When the house falls down, have the Pigs run in a circle through the performing space while the Wolves chase after them. An easy way to get this going is for you to start the run. That way, the Pigs and Wolves will follow your lead. It's always good to remind your students that the Wolves do not actually catch the Pigs, so there is no need for students to grab one another during this exercise. After a few circles, have the Wolves return to their seats, since they could not catch the Pigs.*

That night, the Pigs had nowhere to sleep, and they decided that they would need to build a stronger house. The next day, _____ said, "Let's build a house out of sticks!" The other Pigs said, "Yeah!," and they began to build a house out of sticks. Once they were done, they went inside their new stick house."

> *Choose a different student's name to insert this time. Once that child hears his or her name, he or she will know to repeat the line after you. The other Pigs should all respond with a big, excited "Yeah!" Then on your narration, have the Pigs build the house of sticks. When they are done, they can sit down inside the new house again.*

Just as the Pigs were sitting down to dinner, along came the Big Bad Wolf. Again, he knocked on the door, and the Pigs asked, "Who is it?" The Wolf said, "Little pigs, little pigs, let me in."

And the Pigs said, "Not by the hair on our chinny chin chins." The Wolf said, "Then I'll huff, and I'll puff, and I'll blow your house in," and he did.

*This will be a repetition for the students, but they will still need your narration and your guidance. Have the Wolves knock again as they did before and have your students repeat the lines after you for each section. Again, the children playing the Wolves should blow as hard as they can.*

The house of sticks fell down and the pigs ran as fast as they could. The Wolf ran his fastest, but again he could not catch them.

*Enjoy your second chase scene as much as you did the first one.*

That night the Pigs had nowhere to sleep and knew that they would have to build an even stronger house. So, the next morning, _____ said, "Let's build a house out of bricks." The other Pigs thought this was a great idea and they said, "Yeah!" So they began to build, and when they were finally finished they sat down inside.

*Select a new student to suggest the brick house and, again, have the other Pigs respond with a big, excited "Yeah!" as you narrate this section. When they are building the brick house, remind your students how heavy bricks are and have them pretend to be lifting these very heavy bricks as they build the final house. When they are finished, have the pigs sit down inside their brick house.*

They were just sitting down to roast some marshmallows in the fireplace, when, all of a sudden, along came the Big Bad Wolf. He knocked on the door and the Pigs asked, "Who is it?" The Wolf said, "Little pigs, little pigs, let me in." And the Pigs said, "Not by the hair on our chinny chin chins." The Wolf said, "Then I'll huff and I'll puff, and I'll blow your house in," and he did — but the house did not fall down. This made the Wolf very angry, so he tried it again. But the brick house would not fall down.

*Your students will enjoy having a make-believe marshmallow roast in their fireplace, so feel free to encourage this little added bit into the story. It also serves to establish the use of the fireplace. When the Big Bad Wolf comes, the story should proceed as it did the previous two times. However, this time when the Wolves blow, the house will not fall down. The Wolves can get angry and put on their angry faces. They may even want to stomp their feet. You can do this with the Wolves or let the children decide how the Wolf gets angry. When he tries again and the house does not fall down, your Pigs can respond by cheering or just putting on their excited faces.*

Then, the Wolf looked up and saw the chimney on the roof. He climbed up the side of the house and onto the roof. He decided to slide down the chimney to get into their brick house. But, as he slid down, the fire that the Pigs lit in the fireplace burned his bottom. He began to holler, and he ran out the front door.

*Have the Wolves climb up the side of this pretend house. You may need to do this action, too.*

*Then, upon your narration, the Wolves can slither down to the ground as though they were sliding down the fireplace. When they hear the part about their bottoms burning, they will hoot and holler and run through the performing space and back to their seats.*

The Pigs shouted, "Hooray!" for they knew that they would never hear from that Big Bad Wolf again. And they lived happily ever after. The end.

*The Pigs can respond with their "hooray" as you finish the narration and end the story.*

Everyone stand up and take a big giant bow.

## FOLLOW-UP ACTIVITIES

Working Together. In this story, the Pigs built their three houses and defeated the Wolf by working together with one another. Introduce the word *cooperation*. An easy way to define it to your students is that cooperation means doing things together. Discuss with your students that some things can be done better by working together rather than by ourselves. You can use the story as an example or you may apply it to the lives of the students, for example, building a sand castle, building with blocks, or even rowing a boat.

Break your students up into groups of three and give each group a set of blocks. Have the students build one of the pigs' houses. This will force them to work together, while encouraging dialogue between your students. When they have finished, you can have a House Show and have each group tell the rest of the students about the house that they made for the pigs. *Note:* For additional "cooperation" activities, please see "The Little Red Hen" on page 35.

Being Nice to Others. The Wolf was not very nice to his neighbors. How can people be nicer to friends and neighbors than the Big Bad Wolf was to those Little Pigs? Discuss the ways that the Wolf was not nice to the Pigs. Ask your students if they can think of anything that he could have done instead. Call each child up to the performing space and have that student knock on a friend's or neighbor's door. When the door is answered, encourage them to say one nice thing to their friend.

What Sounds Yummy to You? The Wolf was after the Pigs because he wanted to eat them. Call each student to the performing space and ask each child what his or her favorite food is. It's a great way to get your students thinking about their own likes and dislikes. Since so many children at this age have already become picky eaters, it's also a good way to encourage them to eat the things that they enjoy. Once they've finished, they can have a pretend picnic made up of all their favorite foods.

# Goldilocks and the Three Bears

## OBJECTIVES

- To engage students through storytelling

- To begin to acknowledge that everyone has likes and dislikes

- To teach students rules about taking things from others

## ROLES FOR STUDENTS TO CHOOSE FROM

| Role | Selling Point for the Students |
| --- | --- |
| Goldilocks | Most like your students; adventurous and jolly |
| Papa Bear | Gets to be a daddy |
| Mama Bear | Gets to be a mommy |
| Baby Bear | Funny and can be melodramatic |

It's important to allow gender switching when the students are choosing their roles, so if a little boy wants to play Goldilocks, or a little girl would like to play Papa Bear, let them. As discussed earlier, there are certain things about particular roles that appeal to a child's sense of play or to a child who is working to discover his or her identity. That's part of what role playing is about.

## STORY SYNOPSIS

Once upon a time, a little girl named Goldilocks was wandering through the forest when she discovered a house that belonged to Three Bears. When no one answered the door, she let herself in. She tried their three bowls of porridge (one was too hot, the next was too cold, and the third was just right). She sat on their three chairs (one was too hard, the next was too soft, and the third was just right). Finally, after trying out their three beds (one was too hard, the next was too soft, and the third was just right), she fell asleep. When the Bears came home, they found that someone had been eating their porridge, sitting in their chairs, and sleeping in their beds. They chased Goldilocks out of the house, and she never returned to that part of the forest again.

# NARRATOR

Once upon a time, there were Three Bears who lived in a big house. They decided to go for a picnic one day.

*Have the Three Bears come to the performing space and begin to pack their lunches for the picnic. Find out what sorts of things each student playing a bear would like to put into this picnic lunch. Send them off on their picnics and back to their seats.*

A little girl named Goldilocks had been wandering through the forest. She was getting hungry and tired.

*Make sure Goldilocks puts on her hungry face and her tired face as she walks throughout the performing space.*

She came to a house and thought that the people inside might give her some food. She knocked on the door, but there was no answer. So she decided to go in.

*As you narrate it, Goldilocks will knock on the door. When she realizes that no one is there, have her carefully open the door to take a peek in.*

Inside, she saw just what she was looking for. She went right to the dining-room table where she saw three bowls of porridge. Goldilocks decided to try them.

*Have Goldilocks taste the first one and make a funny face and say, "Ugh, too hot!" Have her taste the second, make a funny face, and say, "Ugh, too cold!" She should taste the third bowl, smile, and say, "Mmm, just right." Make sure she gobbles up the last one as ravenously as possible (it will usually make all the children laugh and will often help if you do it, too). As always, it's perfectly fine for you to say these lines out loud and for the students to repeat them after you.*

Once Goldilocks was finished, she needed to sit down. She walked to the living room where she saw three big chairs. She decided to try them.

*Have Goldilocks pretend to sit on the first one and reply, "Nah, too hard!" Have her pretend to sit on the second and say, "Nah, too soft!" She should sit on the last one and sigh, "Ah, just right." Suddenly, the chair breaks, and she falls on the floor.*

Goldilocks was getting sleepy. She walked upstairs and found three beds. She decided to try them out.

*Make sure Goldilocks pretends to walk up the stairs as you narrate — you may have to act it out with her. Have her lie down on all three beds with the same responses as above. Once she finds the bed that is "just right," she falls asleep. She can lie there during the rest of the story or return to her seat until the Bears discover her.*

The Bears came home from their picnic and were shocked at what they saw.

*The Bears should walk into the house and put on their shocked faces. (Again, you may have to make these faces with them, but they will enjoy it).*

They walked into the dining room.

*Papa Bear says, "Someone's been eating my porridge." Mama Bear says, "Someone's been eating my porridge." Baby Bear says, "Someone's been eating my porridge, and they ate it all up!" Make sure he follows it with a big, silly crying episode (the children will usually laugh and think it's funny).*

Then, they walked into the living room.

*Guide them to the same place that Goldilocks had pretended the chairs were. Papa Bear says "Someone's been sitting in my chair." Mama Bear says "Someone's been sitting in my chair." Baby Bear says, "Someone's been sitting in my chair, and they broke it," followed by a big, silly crying episode.*

The Bears walked upstairs to see what they would find.

*Have them walk up the stairs as you did with Goldilocks. Papa Bear says, "Someone's been sleeping in my bed." Mama Bear says, "Someone's been sleeping in my bed." Baby Bear says, "Someone's been sleeping in my bed, and there she is!" At this point, if your Goldilocks went to sit down, bring her back to the performing space to take her spot in the bed.*

Goldilocks screamed and ran down the stairs, through the living room, and out the door. The Bears tried to chase her, but they couldn't catch her in time.

*Chase scenes are like a big game of tag to children, and they love it. Let the bears chase Goldilocks for a few seconds (going in circles around the performing space usually works best). They'll know to stop running when you say that the Bears couldn't catch her in time. Goldilocks should end the chase by returning to her seat.*

Goldilocks got away and she made sure never to return to that part of the forest ever again. The end.

Everyone stand up and take a big giant bow.

# FOLLOW-UP ACTIVITIES

**Likes and Dislikes.** In the story, Goldilocks tastes three different types of porridges, sits on three chairs with various feelings, and tries out three beds that feel different to her. Discuss this with your students. It's a great way to encourage them to make their own choices, since many of their likes and dislikes may be driven by what their friends think or like (yes, even at this age). Call each child up to the performing space and ask how he or she would like his or her porridge (hot, cold, or medium) and bed (soft, hard, or medium).

You can also expand this exercise beyond the story by asking them about other likes and dislikes (colors, foods, songs, and so on). The key is to get them to speak for themselves and to feel comfortable speaking in front of their peers.

**Taking Things from Others.** In this story, Goldilocks does something not OK: She takes food from the bears and uses their chairs and beds without asking. Discuss this with your students and put it in terms that make sense to them. For example, talk about grabbing toys away from other children or eating things from other children's lunches at school. It's a great way for you to address specific issues that may be going on in your school or with your students. Call each child up to the performing space and give that student an example of what you've just discussed with the group. Ask him or her if it's OK to take things from others (obviously, the answer should be no). It may start to seem repetitive to do this with each child, but repetition is the way children learn.

**What Do Bears Do?** Do bears really live in houses like in this story? Do they really go on picnics and talk to each other? Discuss where bears really live and what kinds of foods they eat. Have all the students come into the performing space and let them all pretend to be bears. They will automatically start roaring and trying to intimidate one another. Point out to your students that bears do other things as well. They climb trees, eat berries and honey, and play with each other. Help them to explore these aspects of a bear's life.

# The Gingerbread Man

## OBJECTIVES

- To start a dialogue about teasing others

- To encourage creativity

- To promote an interest in food

## ROLES FOR STUDENTS TO CHOOSE FROM

| Role | Selling Point for the Students |
| --- | --- |
| Old Lady | Gets to act like a grandmother |
| Old Man | Gets to act like a grandfather |
| Gingerbread Boy | Runs away from everyone and teases them |
| Horse | Gets to act like a horse |
| Cow | Gets to act like a cow |
| Farmer | Does mowing and raking |
| Fox | Is sneaky, the bad guy |

It's perfectly fine to not have two grandparents in this story. If none of your students are interested in playing the Old Man, the lesson will function without missing a beat. In addition, the roles of the Horse, Cow, and Farmer can be flexible in this story. If your students would like to be different animals or characters, this is a great story to indulge their desires; it doesn't really matter if it's a Dog, Chicken, or Alien who wants to eat the Gingerbread Boy. The students will still get to be a part of the story and learn from it

## STORY SYNOPSIS

Once upon a time, there was a little Old Lady and a little Old Man who had no children. They were very lonely without kids around. One day the Old Lady had an idea to make a Gingerbread Boy to have as a son. She and her husband made some dough, rolled it out, shaped it like a boy, and decorated it. They stuck it in the oven and watched it grow. But, when they took the Gingerbread Boy out of the oven, he jumped off the tray and ran out the door. They tried to chase him, but they couldn't catch him. Soon the Gingerbread Boy passed a Cow, a Horse, and a Farmer who all wanted to eat him. One by one, the Gingerbread Boy teased them and then ran away. Finally, the Gingerbread Boy came to a Fox, and he ran from the Fox, too. But the Fox told the Gingerbread Boy that he wouldn't bother him. When the Gingerbread Boy came to a river that needed to be crossed, the Fox offered to help. The Gingerbread Boy climbed on the Fox's tail as the Fox began to swim across the river. But the Fox's tail was sinking, so he asked the Gingerbread Boy to climb onto his back. Soon, his back was sinking, so he asked the Gingerbread Boy to climb onto his nose. When they got to shore, the Fox opened his mouth very quickly and ate half the Gingerbread Boy. When the Fox opened his mouth again, he finished eating the rest of him. And the Gingerbread Boy couldn't tease anyone after that.

## NARRATOR

Once upon a time there was a little Old Lady and a little Old Man who had no children. They were very lonely without kids around. One day the Old Lady had an idea to make a Gingerbread Boy into a son. She and her husband made some dough, rolled it out, shaped it like a boy, and decorated it. They stuck it in the oven and watched it grow.

> *Call the Old Lady and the Old Man to the performing space as you introduce them. When you narrate about how lonely they were, the students should put on their sad faces. Have the Old Lady or Old Man say, "I have an idea. Let's make a little boy out of dough!" Once they start to make him, the students can follow your directions as to how the Gingerbread Boy gets made. You may want to call your Gingerbread Boy to the performing space to start off as the piece of dough. Then the Old Lady and Old Man can shape him how they like. When they stick him in the oven, the student playing the Gingerbread Boy can slowly grow out of the ground into a life-size boy.*

But, when they took him out of the oven, he jumped off the tray and ran out the door. They tried to chase him, but they couldn't catch him.

> *As the Old Lady and Old Man open the oven door, have the Gingerbread Boy jump out of the oven and run away (around the room in a circle usually works best for chase scenes). The Old Lady and Old Man should run after him (in the same direction). As they're running, the Gingerbread Boy says, "Run, run, as fast as you can! You can't catch me, I'm the Gingerbread Man!" and he gets away. (As always, remember to break this line up into small chunks so that your student can repeat it after you.) Have the students playing the Old Lady and Old Man return to their seats.*

Soon the Gingerbread Boy passed a Cow. The Cow asked him to stop because he wanted to eat the Gingerbread Boy. But the Boy just kept on running and teased the Cow as the Cow ran after him.

> *Call the student playing the Cow to the performing space. Let that student roam around a little bit and play up his or her cow-ness. As the Gingerbread Boy approaches the Cow, he should stop while the Cow says, "Please stop little Boy. I would like to eat you and see how you taste." The Gingerbread Boy can stick out his tongue or make a face and then begin to run away. As the*

*Cow chases him (in a circle again, continuity works best), the Gingerbread Boy will say again, "Run, run, as fast as you can! You can't catch me, I'm the Gingerbread Man," and he gets away again. Have the Cow return to his or her seat.*

Then he came to a Horse. The Horse also asked him to stop because the Horse wanted to eat him. But the Gingerbread Boy continued to run. The Horse tried to chase him, but he too could not catch the Gingerbread Boy.

*Have the student playing the Horse come to the performing space. As the Gingerbread Boy approaches the Horse, the Horse will say, "Please stop, little Boy. You look good to eat, and I would like to taste you." Again, the Gingerbread Boy should stick out his tongue to tease the Horse and begin to run away. As the Horse chases him, again the Boy will repeat, "Run, run, as fast as you can! You can't catch me, I'm the Gingerbread Man!" as he gets away from the Horse. Have the Horse return to his or her seat.*

Next, he came to a Farmer. The Farmer wanted to eat that Gingerbread Boy very much, but the Boy just kept on running and teasing the Farmer, too.

*Call the Farmer to the performing space. Repeat the same scenario with the Farmer as with the Cow and the Horse. It may seem redundant to keep repeating the same thing, but the students learn through repetition, and they will enjoy knowing how each part should follow.*

Finally, he came to a Fox, and the Boy ran from the Fox, too. But the Fox told the Gingerbread Boy that he didn't want to bother the Gingerbread Boy.

*Call the Fox to the performing space. As the Gingerbread Boy begins to run from the Fox, have the Fox say, "I don't want to bother you." The Gingerbread Boy can say "thanks" and skip away.*

When the Boy came to a river that needed to be crossed, the Fox offered to help. The Gingerbread Boy climbed on the Fox's tail as the Fox began to swim across the river. But the Fox's tail was sinking, so he asked the Boy to climb onto his back. Soon his back was sinking, so he asked the Boy to climb onto his nose. When they got to shore, the Fox opened his mouth very quickly and ate half the Gingerbread Boy. When he opened his mouth again, he finished eating the rest of him.

*Show the Gingerbread Boy where the river is and as you narrate it, he should stop in front of it and scratch his head, thinking of how to cross. The Fox can come over and say, "I can help!" and then lie down as though he were going to swim across. The child playing the Fox should not physically carry the Gingerbread Boy across the river. The easiest way to create this illusion is for the student playing the Fox to lie down flat, and the Gingerbread Boy can stand next to him or straddle over him. Proceed in whichever way is most safe and comfortable for you. Once the Fox eats him, both the Gingerbread Boy and the Fox can return to their seats.*

And the Gingerbread Boy couldn't tease anyone after that. The end.

Everyone stand up and take a big giant bow.

## FOLLOW-UP ACTIVITIES

### Teasing Others.
In this story, the Gingerbread Boy does something that's not nice: He teases other people and animals and sticks his tongue out at them. Discuss this with your students and talk about why this is not good. Encourage your students to recognize how the Gingerbread Boy could have used nice words instead of teasing the others. Call each student up to the performing space and ask him or her what he or she could do instead of teasing the animals and people in this story. You can flip this activity around a bit and also ask your students what to do if someone is teasing them. Should they hit that person? Should they tease them back? Should they walk away and tell a teacher? Can they use their words? The repetition of this activity will really drill the idea into their heads that teasing is not a good way to make friends.

### For the Love of Food.
Can our food really get up and run? Can it speak? What things can food really do? Pose these questions to your students. Ask them what food really can do for them. It can make them healthy and give them vitamins. It can taste good. Have each student come to the performing space and tell the class what his or her favorite food is. Then have that student take on the shape of this food (spaghetti can wriggle around like a snake, broccoli can stand like a tree, and so on) and run around the room like that food. It's a silly activity, and the children will definitely get a laugh out of it. But the activity will also serve as an incentive to find a food that each student enjoys. This is important at an age when most children are beginning to reject a lot of foods.

### Baking Fun.
How do cookies really get made? What's in them and what makes them grow? Ask your students if any of them have baked cookies before. If some have, ask them if they remember any of the ingredients. Once you've established that cookies are basically made from flour, sugar, and butter, have all the students come to the performing space. It's time to bake! Make sure they all put on their imaginary aprons and chef's hats and make sure they all wash their hands in imaginary sinks around the space. After you establish a giant bowl in the center of the room, have everyone dump in the ingredients and stir with their giant spoons. Once the dough is made, take it out of the giant bowl and put it on the floor. Since the students have to flatten it out, they can either use a giant rolling pin or, for some added fun, jump up and down on the dough to flatten it out. Finally, cut out a gingerbread man and decorate it. Use everyone's help in lifting it into your pretend oven and watch it grow for a couple of seconds. When you take it out, pour some milk and let everyone chow down on this yummy cookie. Your students will have a blast, and they will learn how cookies are really made.

# The Tortoise and the Hare

## OBJECTIVES

- To teach students about good sportsmanship
- To teach students about perseverance and the importance of trying one's hardest

## ROLES FOR STUDENTS TO CHOOSE FROM

| Role | Selling Point for the Students |
|------|-------------------------------|
| Tortoise | The winner of the race |
| Hare | The fastest animal in the forest |

In this story, the Tortoise and the Hare are the only main characters. This leaves you with two options. The first is to split your students into two groups: one to play the Tortoise and the other to play the Hare. Your second option is to choose one hare and one tortoise and have the rest of your students play whatever animals they wish. These animals will voice their doubts about the Hare and then become the cheering section for the Tortoise during the race. This lesson has been prepared to suit the latter choice, but either way is acceptable and fun for the students.

## STORY SYNOPSIS

Once upon a time a Tortoise and a Hare lived in the same part of the forest. Every day the Hare boasted of how much faster he was than the other animals. After weeks of challenges from the Hare and encouragement from the rest of the animals, the Tortoise finally agreed to race the Hare. As the race began, the Hare took off as fast as he could. He was so sure that he would beat the Tortoise that he stopped to take a nap. Meanwhile, the Tortoise moved as fast as he could (which wasn't very fast at all), passed the sleeping Hare, and won the race. And the Hare never bragged about his great speed ever again.

## NARRATOR

*Before beginning the story, you will want to make it clear to your students that a turtle runs much, much slower than a rabbit so that the race in your story will proceed accordingly.*

Once upon a time there were a Tortoise and a Hare who lived in the same part of the forest. The Hare was always bragging about how fast he was and would show off to the rest of the animals every day, running around and around to prove his speed.

*Call the Tortoise and the Hare to the performing space. Have the Hare say, "I'm the fastest ani-mal in this forest. No one's faster than me!" and have him run around the room as fast as he can a couple of times. The Tortoise can put on his bored face while he watches the Hare show off.*

The Hare's favorite thing to do was to remind the Tortoise that he was much slower than the Hare. One day he even challenged the Tortoise to a race.

*As you narrate it, the Hare should stop in front of the Tortoise and say, "I'm much faster than you. You're the slowest animal here. Let's have a race." The Hare can then hop away back to his seat.*

The other animals in the forest were getting tired of hearing the Hare brag. So they called a meeting one night and told the Tortoise that they thought that he should race the Hare. The Tortoise was a little unsure, but once the others encouraged him and gave him their support, the Tortoise decided to accept.

*Have all the other animals come to the performing space. They can all say together, "We're tired of that rabbit!" As you narrate that a meeting was called, point the students in the direction of the meeting and have them sit in a circle. You can select individual students or have them say as a group "You should race the Hare." The Tortoise should tell them all that he's not sure he can win and the other animals should shout words of encouragement. Feel free to make up as many things for your students to say as you like. The meeting can last a long time or a few moments. The meeting should end with the Tortoise saying "I'll do it!" and the other animals cheering him on. They can all return to their seats.*

The next day, the Tortoise told the Hare that he would race him after breakfast. Both the Hare and the Tortoise ate big healthy breakfasts.

*Call the Hare back to the performing space. The Tortoise should walk over to him and say, "Let's have a race after breakfast." They can shake hands on it and walk to opposite sides of the room to eat. As you narrate that they ate big healthy breakfasts, encourage them (perhaps by exam-ple) to stuff their faces. The students will love to see a big, sloppy scene full of pretend food.*

Then all the animals met at the starting line of the race. As soon as the race began, the Hare took off as fast as he could.

*Call all the students into the performing space and have them stand at a point that you deem best to be the starting line. You can have the animals shout in unison, "On your mark, get set, go!" and have the Tortoise and the Hare take off. Remember, the Hare should really run, but the Tortoise should move in slow motion. As always, running scenes work best if the students are running in a circle in the same direction.*

After a few minutes, the Hare was so far ahead of the Tortoise that he couldn't even see him anymore. Since he was sure that he would win, he decided to find a spot to rest for a while. This short rest turned into a long nap.

*As you narrate, have the Hare lie down in a corner somewhere for his little nap.*

In the meantime, the Tortoise was running as fast as he could (which was not very fast at all). He kept on trying, though. Eventually he passed the spot where the Hare was fast asleep, and he kept on running toward the finish line. The Hare woke up just in time to see the Tortoise crossing the finish line, and the Hare yelled in dismay. As the Tortoise won the race, all the other animals congratulated him.

*Encourage the Tortoise to continue his slow-paced run. When he passes the sleeping Hare, direct him toward the finish line (where the rest of the students are standing). As you narrate, the Hare should wake up and yell "Oh, no!!!" The other animals should cheer and shout "Hooray!" as the Tortoise finishes the race.*

And the Hare never bragged about his great speed again. The end.

Everyone stand up and take a big giant bow.

## FOLLOW-UP ACTIVITIES

Perseverance Goes a Long Way. The Tortoise tried and tried to win the race, even though he didn't think he could do it. And he won! Discuss what perseverance is with your students. You may not need to actually teach them the word (it's a pretty big one for them to wrap their minds around). It's the concept that is most important: The idea of trying as hard as one can.

Call each student to the performing space. Ask him or her to tell you about a time when they thought they wouldn't be able to accomplish something but, after trying many times, were able to do it. This could be as simple as going to the potty, putting their shirt on by themselves, tying their shoes, or drinking from a big-kid cup. You can give them examples to help them get the idea. Let each student have a chance and make sure to emphasize to each of them that when you try your hardest, you can do many things.

Be a Good Sport. In this story, the Hare was very upset when he lost the race. Ask the students, "Have you ever been upset when you lost a game?" Talk about winning and losing with your students. Ask them for examples, or ask them to share their experiences about a time when they played a game and lost. Then discuss the importance of being a good sport. You may want to emphasize that even when a person doesn't win, he or she will have another chance the next time. The most important part is having fun.

It's time for a race! Pair up your students. Explain to them that they will be having a real race, just like the Tortoise and the Hare. Show them the starting line and the finish line, which you may want to mark using blocks or toys. Since your performing space is not likely to be a large area where running in a straight line will take much effort, try some other ideas for your race. For example, you can have your students hop on one foot, walk sideways, or leap like a rabbit toward the finish line. As you call up each pair for their race, it's important to remind them about being a good sport. At the end of the race, have the partners give each other a high-five and say to one another "good race!" before they return to their seats. This will foster good sportsmanship and make sure that your students are all still friends when the race is over.

# The Little Red Hen

## OBJECTIVES

- To present the idea of helping others

- To teach students how bread is made

- To introduce the concept of cooperation

## ROLES FOR STUDENTS TO CHOOSE FROM

| Role | Selling Point for the Students |
| --- | --- |
| Hen | A mommy |
| The Chicks | The Hen's children |
| A Cat | Lazy and catlike |
| A Duck | Lazy and ducklike |
| A Dog | Lazy and doglike |

The Cat, Duck, and Dog are characters that can be changed according to your students' whims. If your students would prefer to be dinosaurs, turtles, elephants, or the like, it's perfectly acceptable to indulge in their fantasies for this story. Also, the roles of the Chicks are not particularly large. You may want to let your students know this before they choose their parts if you think the size of the role will be important to some students. However, always stress to your students that the most important thing is to work together to tell the story.

## STORY SYNOPSIS

Once upon a time a Little Red Hen lived in a farmyard with many other animals. One day she found a grain of wheat. She asked her friends to help her plant it, but nobody would help. After it had grown, she asked her friends to help her thresh it, but no one helped. The next day, she asked her friends to help her take it to the mill to have it turned into flour. But, the others did not help. When it had been turned into flour, the Little Red Hen asked her friends to help her bake the flour into bread. But, again, the others were too lazy to help. Finally, when she asked if anyone would like to help her eat the bread, her friends jumped at the chance. But she would not let them. She told them that since they did not help her make the bread, they did not get to share her bread this time. She clucked and called her little Chicks and shared the bread with them instead. And the other animals who got no bread made sure to lend a helping hand the next time they were asked.

# NARRATOR

Once upon a time there was a Little Red Hen who lived in a farmyard with many other animals.

*Call the Little Red Hen to the performing space, and then have the other animals come up as well. Give them a minute to roam around the space as those animals and to converse with one another. Once they've done that, have all the students, except for the Hen, return to their seats.*

One day, as she was digging in the dirt, the Hen found a grain of wheat. She asked, "Who will help me plant this grain of wheat?" But all the other animals were too lazy to help her.

*As you narrate, the Hen should dig in the dirt with her little legs. When she finds the grain of wheat, she can exclaim, "Look what I found!" Call the Cat, Dog, and Duck to the performing space to take a look at what she found. She should ask the question, "Who will help me plant this grain of wheat?" "The Cat, Duck, and Dog all reply, "Not I." Once all the animals have re- fused, direct them to sit on the opposite side of the performing space as though they were in their houses.*

So she did it herself.

*Direct the Little Red Hen to plant the grain of wheat. She can dig a big hole, drop the grain in, fill it back up with soil, and water it.*

After several days, it had grown tall. The Little Red Hen asked, "Who will help me thresh this stalk of wheat?" But the other animals just sat around in the sun and did not help.

*As you narrate, the Little Red Hen should ask, "Who will help me thresh this stalk of wheat?" From their houses, the animals can say their replies as before.*

So she did it herself.

*Direct the Little Red Hen to thresh a stalk of wheat. You can tell your students that threshing means to take the seeds out of the plant. To make it fun for the Hen, you may suggest that she do this with her beak since Hens don't have hands. The students will enjoy watching her peck at it with her nose.*

The next day, the Little Red Hen asked, "Who will help me take the grain to the mill to have it turned into flour?" Again, the others did not help.

*As you narrate, the Hen will ask the question. Again, have the other animals reply as before.*

So, she made the journey herself.

*Have the Hen take a walk around the room. It may be fun to have her give the wheat to you. You then put it through an imaginary machine at the mill and return it to her as a bag of flour.*

When it had been turned into flour, the Little Red Hen was ready to bake. She asked, "Who will help me bake this flour into bread?" And still the animals would not help her.

*As you narrate, the Hen will ask the question. And once more, from their houses, the other animals will give their replies.*

So, the Little Red Hen baked up some delicious-smelling bread all by herself.

*Have the Little Red Hen pour her flour into a bowl and add water, yeast, and sugar. Have her stir it around with her beak and then pour it into a pan. Finally, she should put it into an oven.*

Later that day, the Little Red Hen asked, "Who will help me eat this bread?" This time the other animals jumped at the chance to help her. But she would not let them. She told them that since they did not help her make the bread, they did not get to share her bread this time.

*Have the Hen repeat the question as you narrate it. The Cat, Duck, and Dog should jump up, as you narrate, and run over to the Hen. They can yell "me, me, me" to try to get some bread. Have the Hen say, "No, you will not have bread. You did not help, so you do not get to share!" After this, you can send the other animals either back to their houses or back to their seats.*

She clucked and called her little Chicks and shared the bread with them.

*Have her call her Chicks, as you narrate. Call the Chicks to the performing space and let them gobble up all the yummy bread. They can make noises, such as "mmm," to show how good it is.*

And the other animals, who got no bread, made sure to lend a helping hand the next time they were asked. The end.

Everyone stand up and take a big giant bow.

## FOLLOW-UP ACTIVITIES

**Helping Others.** In this story, the Cat, Duck, and Dog do not get to eat any of the Hen's bread because they would not help her make it. Discuss with your students why it's important to help friends. You may want to stress that by helping someone who needs help, they will have a friend when they need help.

Call each student up to the performing space and ask each child for an example of how to help his or her friends. With this activity it's best not to offer examples for your students.

Let them be creative and use their minds. Each will come up with an endearing way to help a friend.

**Baking Bread.** Bread can be very yummy to eat. Do the students like to eat bread? Talk with your students about the process of making bread. Review the steps that the Hen took in the story to make her bread. Then tell your students that there are many different kinds of bread. Give them examples, such as cinnamon raisin bread, banana bread, and so on. Ask your students if they've ever tried any of these and whether they liked them or not.

It's baking time! Have all your students come into the performing space to make some bread. Explain that they will each be making their own loaf of bread and that they will each get to add an extra ingredient to it (just like the breads you talked about). All the children should put on their aprons and wash their hands in the imaginary sinks. Then, have them dump their flour into their bowls; tell them to add some sugar, water, and yeast. Then they get to stir in their new ingredient. Explain to them that it can be anything from bananas to cotton candy. The students should then pour their mixtures into loaf pans and carefully put them into the oven to watch them bake. When they take them out, have everyone sit in the middle of the room in a circle. Ask each student what kind of bread he or she made. Let the students try each other's bread and share with each other. Be sure to follow your taste testing with big glasses of milk to wash down all that bread.

**We'll Do It Together.** If all the animals had worked together in this story, the Hen would have been able to make the bread much quicker. When people work together, it's called cooperation. Introduce the word *cooperation* to your students. (Even if you have taught them this word before when doing "The Three Little Pigs," you will want to go over it again. Odds are some of the students will need to have their memories refreshed.) Have them repeat the word after you a few times to get used to it. An easy definition for them to understand is that cooperation means doing things together. Ask them to give you examples of times when they can cooperate with their friends.

Make a cooperation machine. To do this, call a student up to the performing space and have him or her do a sound and a movement, something that they can repeat. Then, one by one, you will call up the other students and each will add his or her own sound and movement. Once every child is a part of the activity, they will have made a cooperation machine with everyone working together. Explain that in a real machine, if one part is taken out the whole machine stops. Try doing this with your machine. Take a child out and have the machine stop working. When you add the child back in, the machine can begin to operate again. You can also experiment with slowing it down or speeding it up. This activity is a great way for your students to begin to comprehend how cooperation works and to actually feel it in their bodies.

Don't worry if they all start doing the same sounds and movements after a while. The idea is just for them to be doing something together as a group and to enjoy the experience.

# King Midas and the Golden Touch

## OBJECTIVES

- To introduce the concept of greed
- To get students thinking about people they appreciate
- To encourage students to have hopes and dreams

## ROLES FOR STUDENTS TO CHOOSE FROM

| Role | Selling Point for the Students |
| --- | --- |
| King Midas | Gets to act like a king |
| His Daughter, Marigold | Gets to act like a princess |
| His Dogs | Gets to play an animal |
| A Fairy | Can fly and grant wishes |

In this story, you can add any character that your students would like to play (a mother, a cat, a prince) as long as you establish in the story that these characters are very important to the King. If you do add characters, just add them into the section involving the Princess and the Dogs.

## STORY SYNOPSIS

Once upon a time, a greedy King named Midas wanted all the gold he could possibly have. When a Fairy visited him, offering to grant any wish, he wished that everything he touched would turn to gold. The Fairy granted this wish and put a spell on him. Soon he had turned his food and his family into gold by accident. Frustrated and sad, King Midas went to see the Fairy again. She gave him a magical pitcher of water to sprinkle on his newly turned gold that would return everything back to the way it had been before the spell. He learned his lesson and decided to spend less time with his gold and more time with his loved ones.

## NARRATOR

Once upon a time, in a far off kingdom, there lived a king named King Midas. King Midas was very, very rich. He spent most of his days with his gold, counting it and polishing it. But he wanted more.

*Have King Midas come to the performing space. As you narrate, he can sit down, count his gold, and polish it (you may need to do this with your student, so he gets the idea). After you narrate that he wanted more, have King Midas say, "I wish I had more gold."*

One night, as he was sitting in his room, a fairy came in through the window. When she told the King that she was there to grant him one wish, King Midas told the Fairy that he wished that everything he touched would turn to gold. The Fairy tried to warn the King that this would be an unwise choice, but since this was the King's only wish, the fairy granted it for him.

*Have the student playing the Fairy fly into the performing space and continue around the room a few times. After all, probably one of the main reasons your student chose to be the Fairy was to fly! Once your Fairy has stopped beside the King, have her say, "I'm here to grant you one wish." The King should reply, "I wish everything I touched would turn to gold." As she grants the wish, your Fairy can wave her magic wand to make it come true. Once she's finished, she can fly back to her seat.*

The next morning, when King Midas woke up, he decided to try out his new power. He gently touched the bed, and it turned to gold. He went over to a table and chair, and when he touched them, they turned to gold, too. He was very excited.

*Have King Midas stretch his arms as though he has just woken up (again, you may need to do this with the student). As you narrate, you can point to where the various objects are so that King Midas can touch them. Make sure he puts on his excited face as you narrate this section.*

But when he went to breakfast and tried to drink from a cup, the cup turned to gold and no water came out. The same thing happened to a piece of bread that he picked up to eat. Now the King was getting frustrated.

*Have King Midas move to a new section of the performing space as he goes to breakfast. As you narrate, he should pretend to take a drink from a glass and try to eat a piece of bread. You'll definitely want to see his frustrated (or angry) face for this part.*

Soon, his Dogs came in to greet him. As King Midas bent down to pet them, the Dogs froze in place and turned to gold as well. The King thought this was terrible. Finally, the Princess entered the room and as the King leaned over to kiss her cheek, she froze and turned to gold, too.

*Call the Dogs into the performing space. Give them a few moments to romp around the way that dogs do. But as soon as the King tries to pet them, they should all freeze. They will understand this from your narration. The Princess will come to the performing space as you announce her. You may want to give her a moment to skip around the room. Then, as the King leans to kiss her on the cheek, she should freeze, too. If your students are too shy for a kiss on the cheek, you can substitute it with a handshake, a high-five, or nothing at all. The students will understand what has taken place in the story because of your narration. Have your students stay in their frozen positions.*

King Midas called the Fairy's name and begged her to return. When the Fairy returned, the King told her that he had learned his lesson. He did not want everything to be gold. He never wanted to see gold again. He just wanted his loved ones to return to their old selves. The Fairy, having seen that the King had learned his lesson, gave him a pitcher to fill with water. She told the King to sprinkle this magical water on everything that had turned to gold and all would return to normal.

*Have King Midas call to the Fairy by simply calling out, "Fairy, come back!" The Fairy should fly into the space again and ask the King, "What's wrong?" The King can say, "I want it back to normal. I learned my lesson." As you narrate it, have the Fairy give King Midas a pitcher to fill. She can tell him, "Sprinkle this on everyone." Then she should fly back to her seat again.*

King Midas ran through the castle sprinkling the water on anything and anyone he had touched. When the Princess and his Dogs came to life, he was very excited to see them. They all sat down to breakfast and ate together.

*The King should run through the performing space sprinkling the magical water on everyone. Once they have been touched, each person can come back to life and unfreeze. To add some excitement to this part, they can all cheer "hooray!" when they are all unfrozen. As you narrate, have the King, the Princess, and the Dogs all sit down in the center of the room to eat a big breakfast.*

And the King decided to spend more of his time with his loved ones and much less of his time with his gold. And they lived happily ever after. The end.

Everyone stand up and take a big giant bow.

## FOLLOW-UP ACTIVITIES

**Being Greedy.** In this story, King Midas has lots of gold already, but he wants more. Introduce the word *greedy* to your students. A simple definition is someone who is greedy has lots and lots of something but still wants more and won't share it with others. Discuss it in terms that make sense to them. For example, describe someone who has more chocolate than anyone else but refuses to share, or a person who wants all the toys in the toy store for himself. Ask your students to think of some examples and share them with the class.

Have all your students come to the performing space. Give each student his or her own space in the room. Tell them that each is filled with something special. You may tell one child that her space is filled with chocolate chip cookies or another that his space is filled with puppy dogs. Once each child has his or her own space and a special thing, it's time to share. Explain to the students that it would be greedy to keep all these things for themselves. Encourage them to pick up their imaginary "share baskets" and walk around the performing space, sharing their special objects with the rest of the class. Once they've got enough special objects to satisfy themselves, they can return to their space and play with all their new things. When they've had a couple of minutes to play with their imaginary objects, have them walk around the room giving the other students high-fives to thank them. This activity will help your students to further understand what the word *greedy* means. In addition it will promote sharing.

## Appreciation.

In this story, the King doesn't want the Princess or his Dogs to be turned to gold because he loves them too much. Explain to your students that if the King hadn't unfrozen the Princess, he never would have been able to talk to her or play with her again. Discuss why it's important to care about people.

Call each student to the performing space individually. Ask them to tell you one person who they definitely wouldn't want to turn to gold. It may be their mother or father, it could be a friend, or it might be their cat. The important thing is to help your students recognize one person who they love and appreciate. This activity is not about making them choose between one parent or another, or one friend over another. If a student comes up with a whole list of people, let them ramble on about those individuals. It's lovely to hear a child share who he or she cares about.

## When You Wish Upon a Star.

King Midas wished for more gold. What would each student wish for? Sit in a circle with your students and discuss this with them. Explain that people make wishes all the time in real life. Sometimes they come true, and other times they don't. But it's always important to have hopes and dreams.

It's time to grant wishes! Go around the circle and ask each child what his or her wish would be if the Fairy came to their room. Once they've told you, wave your imaginary wand and grant their wish. Give them a minute or two to explore what you've just granted them by letting them leave the circle. For example, if a child wishes he could fly, let him fly around the room for a few moments. Or if another student wishes to be a ballerina, let her dance through the space. Once everyone has had a chance, wave your wand and have them all fly back to their seats together. This activity is a great way to stimulate your students' imaginations and to get them thinking about their own hopes and wishes.

# Little Red Riding Hood

## OBJECTIVES

- To begin a dialogue with students about the dangers of talking to strangers

## ROLES FOR STUDENTS TO CHOOSE FROM

| Role | Selling Point for the Students |
| --- | --- |
| Little Red Riding Hood | Gets to act like an adventurous girl |
| Her Mother | Gets to act like a mommy |
| The Wolf | Gets to act like the bad guy |
| Grandmother | Gets to act like a grandmother |
| Woodcutter | Gets to act strong and courageous, saves Little Red Riding Hood and Grandma |

## STORY SYNOPSIS

Once upon a time there was a girl named Little Red Riding Hood. One day, Little Red Riding Hood went to visit her Grandma. On her way there, she met a hungry Wolf that wanted to eat her. When she told him where she was going, he ran there quickly and got to her Grandma's house first. Grandma had heard the Wolf coming and was hiding in a closet. The Wolf came into the house through the chimney and disguised himself to look like Grandma. As Little Red Riding Hood arrived and was let into the cottage, she slowly began to notice that her Grandmother looked and sounded a bit different. The Wolf took off his disguise and was about to eat her, when a woodcutter who had been working nearby came through the door to save her. He waved his axe, but the Wolf was able to escape out the door. As soon as it was safe, Little Red Riding Hood's Grandmother came out from the closet where she had been hiding. The Wolf made sure not to return to that part of the forest again, they both thanked the Woodcutter for saving them from the Wolf, and they all lived happily ever after.

## NARRATOR

Once upon a time there lived a little girl who lived near a forest. She had a special red riding coat with a hood that she wore all the time. Because of this, most people called her Little Red Riding Hood.

*Call Little Red Riding Hood to the performing space and let her skip around the room for a moment. As you narrate, you may want to have the student put on her red riding coat, or you can save that part for when she is about to leave the house. It's also fine to do it both times.*

One day, Little Red Riding Hood's Mother gave her a basket of cakes and butter to bring to her Grandmother who lived in another town. Her Grandmother was feeling sick, and this was meant as a gift for her. Before leaving, Little Red Riding Hood's Mother warned her not to stop and talk to strangers on the way, as she was often known to do. She put on her red coat, kissed her Mother good-bye, and left for her Grandmother's cottage.

*Have the Mother enter the performing space as you begin this section. She can hand a basket to Little Red and say, "Take these to your Grandma. She's not feeling well." After Little Red Riding Hood says, "All right," the Mother should warn her, "And remember, don't talk to strangers on the way." Then, as you narrate, Little Red Riding Hood will put on her red riding coat, kiss her mother good-bye, and skip out the door. The Mother can return to her seat.*

On the way there she met a Wolf that wanted to eat her. He could not eat her now for fear that someone might see. So he asked her where she was going. She told him that she was going to her Grandmother's house and showed him where it was. Then she continued on her way.

*Call the Wolf to the performing space as Little Red Riding Hood continues to skip. He can watch her for a moment and perhaps even lick his lips. Have her stop in front of him as he asks, "Where are you going, little girl?" Little Red Riding Hood should reply, "I'm going to my Grandmother's house. She lives near the mill." She can continue to skip around and can eventually skip back to her seat.*

The Wolf took off for Grandmother's house to make it there before the little girl. When he got there, he disguised his voice to sound like Little Red Riding Hood's, but the Grandmother did not believe it. Hearing the Wolf coming in through the chimney, the Grandmother quickly hid in a closet.

*Let the Wolf run around the space for a moment as he is hurrying to Grandmother's house. Once he's there, call the Grandmother to the space and let her lie down where there would be a bed in her house. Have the Wolf knock on the door three times, "knock, knock, knock," and then say, "Granny, it's Little Red Riding Hood." As you narrate, have the Grandmother put on her frightened face and run to a far corner of the room to hide in the closet. After she has done this, she can either stay in that spot until her character appears at the end, or you can direct her back to her seat.*

When the Wolf got inside, he lay down in Grandma's bed and disguised himself to look like her. Little Red Riding Hood arrived and entered the cottage. She slowly noticed that her Grandmother looked and sounded a bit different.

*Have the Wolf slide down to the floor, as though he were climbing down the chimney. Then he can walk over to where Grandmother had been lying in bed and begin to disguise himself. Some things to narrate for him to do include putting on a bonnet, slipping into a nightgown, trying to comb his ears down. Once the Wolf is lying down in bed, call Little Red Riding Hood to the performing space again. She can knock on the door as the Wolf did. When she enters, she should go over to the Wolf and say, "Why Grandma, what big ears you have." The Wolf says, "The better to hear you with." Little Red Riding Hood says, "Why Grandma, what big eyes you have." The Wolf says, "The better to see you with." Little Red Riding Hood says, "Why Grandma, what big teeth you have." The Wolf says, "The better to eat you with." Little Red Riding Hood should definitely put on her surprised or scared face.*

The Wolf took off his disguise and was about to eat her when a Woodcutter who had been working nearby came through the door to save her. He waved his axe, but the Wolf was able to escape out the door.

*When the Woodcutter hears his name, he should jump into the space (you probably won't even need to call him). Let him chase the Wolf around the room a few times (chase scenes are always a blast for the children). After they've completed a couple of circles, and the Wolf hears your narration about escaping out the door, direct the Wolf back to his seat.*

As soon as it was safe, Little Red Riding Hood's Grandmother came out from the closet where she had been hiding. They both thanked the Woodcutter for saving them from the Wolf.

*If the Grandmother went back to her seat, have her return to the space. Otherwise, upon your narration, she can open the imaginary closet door and come over to the Woodcutter and Little Red Riding Hood. Little Red Riding Hood and the Grandmother should say thank you to the Woodcutter.*

The Wolf made sure not to return to that part of the forest again, and Little Red Riding Hood, the Grandmother, and the Woodcutter all lived happily ever after. The end.

Everyone stand up and take a big giant bow.

## FOLLOW-UP ACTIVITIES

**Talking to Strangers.** In this story, Little Red Riding Hood talked to the Wolf in the forest on the way to her Grandmother's. Did she know him? Or was he a stranger? This lesson is a very delicate one because of the age group and the subject matter of this lesson. However, it's important for preschool-aged students to know what a stranger is and how to deal with strangers.

Discuss the opening statement and the questions to this activity with your students. Help your students understand that since Little Red Riding Hood did not know the Wolf, he was a stranger to her. Ask them if they think it's OK to talk to strangers and then ask them why. It's important to let them know that most strangers are good, but others are Danger Strangers. You may want to compare Danger Strangers to bad guys in cartoons, or you may simply want to discuss how some adults are not always nice.

Once you've established what a stranger is, it's then important to identify good strangers or people that it's always OK to talk to, such as policemen, firemen, and people behind the counter at a store. Call each student to the performing space and ask him or her who he or she would talk to if the child needed help. This activity is mainly to put emphasis on good strangers, but it will also be fun for most of your students to pick a store clerk, policeman, or fireman, since many are heroes to them.

Since this is such an important issue, you may want to get the parents involved in this dialogue if you find it would be appropriate and acceptable to do in your school or learning center. You can send a note home to the parents letting them know the nature of your drama lesson, what was talked about, and some additional things to talk about with their children, such as emergency phone numbers or what to do if a stranger approaches the child.

## Picnic Time.
Since this is such a serious lesson, it's fun to end it with an activity that is light and fun. Sit in a circle with your students. Go around the circle and ask each student to put one thing into the picnic basket that he or she would want to send along to Grandma.

Once your imaginary picnic basket has been filled, have the students all put on their riding coats (they can choose what color theirs are) and take a walk in the woods to get Grandma. You may want to stop and pick some flowers along the way. Tell your students to wait there for a moment as you leave the room momentarily to get Grandma. Reenter the space as Grandma and continue on your way with the children. (No costume is necessary. A slight change in voice will be enough for them to simply go along for the ride.) Then have all the students help you to lay out your enormous picnic blanket and take out all the things that the students chose to put in. Have a picnic and enjoy! You'll, of course, want to make sure that you drop Grandma back at home and return as yourself before the end of the lesson.

# The Story of Peter Pan

## OBJECTIVES

- To encourage students to use their words instead of fighting
- To help students identify what makes them happy
- To indulge in the land of make-believe

## ROLES FOR STUDENTS TO CHOOSE FROM

| Role | Selling Point for the Students |
| --- | --- |
| Peter Pan | A young boy who can fly |
| Wendy | Nurturing, like a mommy |
| John | An older brother |
| Michael | The youngest child |
| Captain Hook | The bad guy |
| Tinkerbell | A fairy |
| The Lost Boys | Many little boys who like adventures |
| Tiger Lily | An Indian |

There are many characters in this story. It's great if you can fill all the roles, but it's not vital to the story. The most important characters are Peter Pan, Wendy, and Captain Hook. The rest can be removed at your discretion.

## STORY SYNOPSIS

Once upon a time a young girl named Wendy woke up to find a boy called Peter Pan in her room. He was looking for his shadow. She helped him to find it and sewed it back on for him. Peter Pan taught Wendy and her brothers, John and Michael, how to fly and took them to his home in Never-Never Land. There he introduced them to his friends, the Lost Boys, and saved his friend Tiger Lily from the evil Captain Hook. After a few days in Never-Never Land, Wendy, John, and Michael feared that their parents would miss them. So Peter Pan led the way and flew them home. And they all promised to return to Never-Never Land to see Peter Pan again.

# NARRATOR

Once upon a time there lived a girl named Wendy who had two brothers, John and Michael.

*Have Wendy, John, and Michael come to the performing space and skip around and play for a moment to establish who their characters are.*

One night, while they were sleeping soundly in their rooms, the window opened. In flew a boy and a fairy. The boy was searching the room for something. When he couldn't find it, he began to cry.

*As you narrate that they were sleeping, Wendy, John, and Michael should lie down on the floor and pretend to sleep. Upon your narration, have Peter Pan and Tinkerbell fly into the performing space. They have probably chosen these roles, in part, so that they can fly. So let them fly around the space for a moment or two before moving on. Then make sure that Peter Pan and Tinkerbell look around the space in search of Peter Pan's shadow. As you narrate, Peter Pan should sit down and cry (or put on his sad face). You may need to do this with him if he is too embarrassed or finds it too silly.*

Wendy woke up and saw the boy sitting in her room crying. When she asked him why, he told her that he couldn't find his shadow. She helped him, and together they found it and sewed it back on to him.

*Wendy should wake up as you narrate. She can say to Peter Pan, "Boy, why are you crying?" Peter Pan can stop crying and say to her, "I can't find my shadow." As you narrate, the two of them should begin to search the performing space for his shadow. When they find it, you may need to help Wendy to mime the sewing. Most children this age do not quite understand how to sew. But, by watching you, she will get the idea. Once the shadow is sewn on, let Peter Pan stand up and admire himself for a moment.*

The boy told Wendy that his name was Peter Pan and that he and his fairy, Tinkerbell, had flown from Never-Never Land. He taught Wendy, John, and Michael how to fly by sprinkling fairy dust on them and asking them to think happy thoughts. Then Peter Pan invited them to fly to Never-Never Land with him.

*Peter Pan should introduce himself by saying, "My name is Peter Pan. And this is my fairy, Tinkerbell." Teaching them how to fly simply involves Peter Pan telling the others to think happy thoughts while Tinkerbell sprinkles some fairy dust over the children. Then let your happy children fly around the room a few times. Children love the idea of flying, and this is a wonderful way to indulge them in one of their fantasies. As you narrate, have Peter Pan say, "Would you like to come to Never-Never Land with me?" Wendy, John, and Michael can all cheer "yeah!" as they fly away to Never-Never Land.*

When they got there, Peter Pan's best friends, the Lost Boys, greeted them. The Lost Boys had never had a girl around and were very happy when Wendy arrived. She liked to take care of them and read them books at bedtime.

*Everyone who is flying should stop when you narrate that they arrived in Never-Never Land. (You may need to point to a place for them to stop.) As you mention their names, the Lost Boys should come into the space and say "hi" to the newcomers. Wendy can take care of the Lost Boys by washing their hair, feeding them big meals, and finally reading them a bedtime story as they sit around and listen. You can even have them all fall asleep for a few seconds to have a moment of stillness.*

But, one day, the Lost Boys came back from playing to tell Peter Pan that the evil Captain Hook had kidnapped their good friend, Tiger Lily.

*Have everyone wake up. All the Lost Boys can stand up and say, "Captain Hook has kidnapped Tiger Lily!" At this point, they can all put on their scared faces. After that, everyone except for Peter Pan should return to their seats.*

Peter Pan knew that he had to help Tiger Lily. He flew to Captain Hook's ship to try to save her. There, Captain Hook challenged Peter Pan to a fight. Peter Pan didn't like to fight. So, he flew through the air and confused Captain Hook so much, that soon Captain Hook fell off his ship and into the water. A crocodile came by and gobbled Captain Hook's hand, and Captain Hook was never heard from again.

*Peter Pan should fly around the space for a moment to get to Captain Hook's ship. Once he gets there, call Captain Hook and Tiger Lily to the performing space. Tiger Lily should sit in a corner with her scared face on. If you think it's appropriate, you can have her sit with her hands behind her back, as though she's been tied up. However, this may scare some children, so use your judgment to decide if your student can handle this. Captain Hook does not verbally need to challenge Peter Pan to a fight. The students will understand from your narration that he has done so. The fight can consist of Captain Hook waving his sword and Peter Pan simply flying around the room to avoid Captain Hook. This is the easiest way to perform the duel without encouraging your students to have a sword fight. As you narrate, Captain Hook should fall to the floor, as though he were falling into the water. Once you narrate his demise, you can send Captain Hook back to his seat. It's fun for everyone else to cheer for Peter Pan and Tiger Lily.*

Once Tiger Lily was home safely, it was time for Wendy, John, and Michael to return home. They didn't want their parents to worry about them. So Tinkerbell sprinkled some fairy dust on them and Peter Pan took them home. When they returned to their house, they promised Peter Pan that they would come back to Never-Never Land for some more adventures. Peter Pan flew home.

*Tiger Lily can return to her seat once you've narrated that she was safe. Have Wendy, John, and Michael return to the performing space as you speak about their characters. All three can tell Peter Pan, "It's time for us to go home." Tinkerbell should sprinkle some fairy dust on them, and the students can take flight once more. As you narrate their return home, Wendy, John, and Michael should get back into their beds and say good-bye to Peter. Peter can fly back to his seat.*

Wendy, John, and Michael went to sleep, hoping that they would see their new friends again very soon. The end.

Everyone stand up and take a big giant bow.

## FOLLOW-UP ACTIVITIES

### Using Your Words.
In this story, Captain Hook tries to fight with Peter Pan. Is it OK to fight? What can a person do instead? Discuss this with your students. Ask them why they think Captain Hook wanted to fight with Peter Pan. Most likely they will come up with a myriad of answers ranging from jealousy to meanness. You can accept all these answers as long as your students believe that they are the reasons why Captain Hook wanted to fight with swords. Then ask your students what Captain Hook should have done instead of challenging Peter Pan to a fight. Could he have used words?

Call each child to the performing space and give him or her an example of something that might make a child angry. Some examples include a friend taking away a toy, someone knocking down a tower that a child built, or even one child hitting another. Once you give the student an example, ask the child if he or she should hit someone to solve the problem. Obviously the answer should be no. Then ask your students how they can use their words to solve the problem. You can encourage them to say, "Hey, don't do that," or to even go and tell a teacher. The most important thing to stress is that hitting and fighting with hands is never right.

### Just Think Happy Thoughts.
In this story, the children learn how to fly by thinking happy thoughts. What makes each student happy? Sit in a circle with your students and discuss this. Tell them each to think of something that makes them happy.

It's time to fly! Go around the circle and ask each child what his or her happy thought is. Once the student has told you, sprinkle some fairy dust on him or her, and tell the child it's his or her turn to fly through the room. Let each child fly around the circle a few times before returning to his or her seat. Give everyone a chance to fly. You can end the activity by having the whole class think of their happy thoughts once more and then have them fly back to their seats.

## I Know a Place Called Never-Never Land.

Is Never-Never Land a real place or a make-believe place? Would any students like to go to Never-Never Land? Talk with your students about Never-Never Land and establish with them the difference between a real place and a make-believe place. Let them know that make-believe lands are just as fun to go to; you just have to travel there in your imagination.

Take an imaginary trip to Never-Never Land with all your students. Let them fly (because after all, that is the only way to get there). Once you are in Never-Never Land, show them around for a moment. Indicate to them where the mermaids live, where the pirate ships are, and where the Lost Boys live. Remind them that it's not OK to fight as pirates, and let them know that pirates do other things, like finding treasure and sailing on ships. Then let 'em loose. Tell your students that they will have five minutes to visit all three places in Never-Never Land. They may choose to become some of these characters while they explore. The idea is for them to lose themselves in this land of make-believe and to have a reference to come back to later in their free playtime. When time is up, gather up the students and fly back to school. Let them know that now that they have been to Never-Never Land, they are welcome to go back any time they wish.

# Jack and the Beanstalk

## OBJECTIVES

- To teach students the consequences of taking things from others

- To help students understand how plants grow

- To explore the concept of size

## ROLES FOR STUDENTS TO CHOOSE FROM

| Role | Selling Point for the Students |
|---|---|
| Jack | Gets to act adventurous and brave |
| The Cow | Is fun for anyone who's dying to be an animal |
| Jack's Mother | Gets to act like a mommy |
| The Giant | Gets to act big and strong |
| Strange Old Man | Is the first one to touch the beans |
| The Beanstalk | Gets to grow from a bean into a beanstalk. |

If a student really wants to play a father instead of a mother, it's perfectly fine to either change the role to a father or to add a father to the story. If you choose the second option, just have the mother and father say and do everything together.

## STORY SYNOPSIS

Once upon a time, there lived a boy named Jack and his Mother. They were so poor that they had to sell their cow. When Jack sold this cow, instead of getting money, he received magic beans. But when he showed these to his Mother, she became so angry she threw them out the window. The next morning, Jack woke up to find that the beans had grown into a giant beanstalk that stretched up to the sky. He climbed all the way up and discovered a Giant's palace at the top. Jack took the Giant's gold and ate the Giant's food. When the Giant discovered him, he chased Jack all the way back down the beanstalk. Jack got to the bottom first, chopped down the beanstalk, and the Giant fell to the ground, creating an enormous hole, and the Giant was never heard from again.

# NARRATOR

Once upon a time there was a boy named Jack who lived on a farm with his Mother. His best friend was their cow, Bessie. Jack and Bessie loved to play games together and walk through the fields with one another.

*Call Jack into the performing space and let him skip around for a moment. Then let Bessie, the cow, come into the space. As you narrate the games and activities, they can act them out. For example, you might say that Jack and Bessie loved to run around and play tag together. Then have the two students playing these roles do just that.*

But, one day, Jack's Mother told him that because they didn't have enough money, they would have to sell the cow. Jack was very sad, but he knew he had to do what his Mother said.

*Have Jack's Mother come to the performing space and repeat after you, "Jack, we have to sell the cow." Jack can put on his sad face, or you can have him repeat "No!" after you. After you narrate that Jack knew he had to do what his Mother said, have the Mother return to her seat.*

So Jack took Bessie into town to try to sell her. On the way there, they met a Strange Old Man who wanted to buy a cow. He paid Jack in beans. Jack was angry at first, but the man told him that they were magic beans. Jack couldn't say no to magic beans, so he took them, said good-bye to Bessie, and walked home.

*As you narrate, Jack and Bessie should begin to walk on their journey. As you introduce the Strange Old Man, call the student playing that role into the performing space. Jack can repeat after you, "Would you like to buy a cow?" and the Strange Old Man should say, "Yes." Jack can hold out his hand to receive the money, and the Strange Old Man should give him the magic beans. When he does this, Jack should put on his angry face and say "Beans!" The Strange Old Man should repeat after you, "Not just any beans. These are magic beans." As you continue to narrate the story, Jack should say good-bye to Bessie, and the Strange Old Man and Bessie can return to their seats.*

When Jack showed his Mother the beans, she got so angry that she threw them out the kitchen window and sent Jack to bed without any supper.

*Jack's Mother will come into the performing space when she hears her character mentioned again. Have Jack show her the beans. She will put on her angry face and repeat after you, "Beans!" as Jack tries to calm her by saying, "But they're magic beans!" Have her throw them out the window, and they can both return to their seats as they pretend to sleep.*

That night, while everyone was sleeping, the beans began to grow out of the ground. They grew and grew and grew until they were higher than the trees, up into the sky, and past the clouds.

*If a student wants to play the Beanstalk, this is his or her moment. Have that student come into the space and curl up on the floor in a tight ball, mimicking a seed. As you narrate how the plant began to grow, that child will begin to grow as well. Have them slowly unroll and stand up as tall as he or she can.*

The next morning, when Jack woke up, he looked outside and saw the biggest Beanstalk he'd ever seen. He decided to climb it.

*Jack can yawn and stretch his arms (following your example) and walk back into the performing space. When he does, have him look up at the big Beanstalk. When he decides to climb it, you can pretend with him so he gets the idea.*

When he got to the top he saw an unbelievable sight: a Giant's palace. He walked around inside and saw amazing things. First, he grabbed some of the Giant's gold because he knew he and his Mother needed it. Then he climbed up on the table and began to eat the Giant's food.

*Have him walk around the room and look at all these things. He can pretend to take some gold and put it in his pockets. It's always fun to gobble food and be a big slob about it when pretending. Encourage Jack to eat as much of this big, giant food as possible. You may want to do this with him, as the children will find it funny to see you stuff your face too.*

But, all of a sudden he heard loud footsteps coming. He hid under the table and in came the Giant. The Giant could tell that someone had been there and he began to sniff around with his giant nose. He said, "Fee, Fie, Foe, Fum. I smell the blood of an Englishman." He looked under a chair, but nothing was there. He sniffed again and said, "Fee, fie, foe, fum. I smell the blood of an Englishman." This time he looked under the couch, but no one was there. He sniffed again and said, "Fee, fie, foe, fum. I smell the blood of an Englishman." He looked under the table and saw Jack!

*Jack can hide against a wall or in the middle of the room. (Let the student decide.) The child playing the Giant will most likely stomp into the performing space as you introduce the character into the story. If not, call that student up. The Giant can sniff around and should repeat the lines after you. Each time he does, have him check a different spot until he finds Jack.*

Jack ran back to the Beanstalk and began to climb down as fast as he could. The Giant followed. They raced down to the bottom. Jack got there first, and when he did, he grabbed an axe and began to chop down the Beanstalk. When it finally fell, the Giant fell with it. The Giant made a giant hole in the ground and was never heard from again.

*As you've already learned, there's nothing better to children than the excitement of a chase scene. The faster you speak during this section, the more intense the thrill of the scene will become. The child who played the Beanstalk should hurry back into the space, as Jack pretends to climb down. The Giant can follow and climb down on the other side. Please note that there is no rea-son for the students to be touching or grabbing the child playing the Beanstalk. If they do, gen-tly remind them that this is their friend and not a real Beanstalk. They are not to touch the child. Once you narrate it, Jack will chop down the Beanstalk. The Giant and the Beanstalk will fall to the floor. They can remain there for the rest of the story, or you can have them return to their seats.*

Jack showed his Mother the gold that he had taken, and with that gold they were able to buy back Bessie.

*Jack's Mother will return to the space, and when you narrate it, so will the Strange Old Man and Bessie. Bessie and Jack may want to give each other a high-five because they are happy to see each other again.*

They never worried about money ever again, and they lived happily ever after. The end.

Everyone stand up and take a big giant bow.

## FOLLOW-UP ACTIVITIES

**Can Plants Really Grow That High?** In this story, the beanstalk grew all the way up to the sky. Can a plant really get that big? How do they grow? Take a few moments to discuss these questions with your students. As always, make references to things that they will understand. For example, a flower may not grow very tall, but some trees get to be very big. You may want to compare these examples and begin to discuss some of the similari-ties and differences between a flower and a tree.

Discuss what three things make seeds grow into plants: earth, water, and sunlight. Di-vide your students into three groups. Have the seeds come into the performing space and lie down on the floor in little balls. When you call them, the water will come dancing into the space and dance around the seeds as though they were raindrops or water from a wa-tering can. As they return to their seats, the sunshine will come into the performing space and hold their arms out wide to let all the sun shine down onto the seeds. Continue this cycle and have the seeds slowly grow out of the ground until they are fully grown. This ac-tivity is simple and is a great way for your students to understand the principles of how plants grow.

**Taking Things from Others.** Jack does things that are not good in this story. He takes gold from the Giant without asking, and he eats the Giant's food without asking. Dis-cuss this with your students and put it in terms that they will understand. For example, taking food out of somebody else's lunch box without asking or taking toys out of some-one's cubby without his or her permission are two comparable problems.

Call each student to the performing space and ask him or her if it's OK to take some-thing from a friend without asking (obviously, the answer should be no). Ask that student what he should do if he wants to borrow something from someone. Encourage that child to fully ask a question, such as "Can I play with that please?" Once he or she gives you the answer, give the child a high-five and send the child back to his or her seat. This may seem repetitive to do with each student, but repetition is the way children learn.

**Sizes.** In this story we met a Giant who lives in a giant house and has giant things. If someone is a giant, are they bigger or smaller than you? Discuss some words that are used to identify sizes. When you talk about big things, you can use the words *giant, huge, big,* or *tall*. When you talk about small things, they might know the words *little* or *tiny*. See what words your students can think of.

Go on an exploration of sizes. First, visit a giant house. Have the students eat giant food (grapes the size of their heads), climb up onto giant chairs, or sleep in enormous beds. Then go to a miniature house (like a dollhouse). The students can duck to get through doorways, eat a sandwich like it's a peanut, or curl up in a teeny bed. This is a good way to introduce the concept of size to your students.

# Cinderella

## OBJECTIVES

- To have students think about being nice to others
- To teach students what a responsibility is
- To encourage individuality and creativity

## ROLES FOR STUDENTS TO CHOOSE FROM

| Role | Selling Point for the Students |
| --- | --- |
| Cinderella | Gets to be a princess, meets the Prince |
| Evil Stepmother | Gets to boss people around and act mean |
| Evil Stepsisters | Get to act mean |
| Mice | Make Cinderella's gown, turn into horses |
| Fairy Godmother | Also is like a princess, has a magic wand |
| The Prince | Marries Cinderella and gets to chase her |

Because there are so many roles in this story (and most girls will want to play Cinderella), you may wind up playing many of the roles. As always, this is perfectly acceptable. There are a number of characters with strong personalities, and you should allow the students to gravitate toward the ones that fill a space in their psyche.

## STORY SYNOPSIS

Once upon a time there lived a girl named Cinderella. She lived with her Evil Stepmother and her Evil Stepsisters who made her do chores all day long. One day, they received word that the Prince was giving a ball and that everyone in the kingdom was invited. Cinderella would be allowed to go only if she finished all her extra chores that day. She worked very hard to finish them and then put on a dress that her friends, the mice, had made for her. But when the Stepsisters and Stepmother saw what Cinderella was wearing, they ripped it up, accusing her of making the dress with their fabrics, scarves, and buttons. Cinderella's Fairy Godmother then came and visited her. She gave Cinderella a dress to wear to the ball, changed the mice to horses, and turned a pumpkin into a coach. Cinderella went to the ball and danced with the Prince all night long. When the clock struck twelve, Cinderella had to rush home because the Godmother's spell broke then. All she left behind was a glass slipper. The next day, the Prince went to every house until he found the girl who fit the glass slipper. When he found Cinderella, he brought her to the castle where they were married. And they lived happily ever after.

# NARRATOR

Once upon a time a girl named Cinderella lived in a house with her Evil Stepmother and two Evil Stepsisters. Every day they gave her many, many chores to do, so many that she was almost like a servant.

*Call your Cinderella and your Stepmother and Stepsisters into the performing space. Give some chores for them to call out to Cinderella. For example "Cinderella, mop the floor," "Cinderella, make the beds," "Cinderella, clean the windows." Make sure Cinderella pretends to do all these things.*

One day, a letter from the Prince came. It announced that he was giving a ball. The Evil Stepsisters and Stepmother were very excited about going to the ball. Cinderella wanted to go too, but her Stepmother told her that she couldn't go unless she finished all her chores that day.

*If you like, you can make a big deal about announcing the ball yourself. Enter the space as the town crier and announce, "Hear ye, hear ye, the Prince is inviting everyone to a ball at the castle." The Stepsisters, Stepmother, and Cinderella should put on their excited faces. As you narrate, have the Stepmother tell Cinderella that she must finish her chores before she can go. The Stepmother can even give a mean little laugh afterward.*

When the day came, the Evil Stepmother gave Cinderella even more chores than usual. Cinderella had to work very hard to finish them.

*Have the Stepmother and Stepsisters call out even more chores than before: sweep the floor, wash the dishes, do the laundry, make the dinner. When you are finished with this section, send them all back to their seats.*

Cinderella's best friends, the Mice, had been working hard too. They wanted to make a beautiful dress for Cinderella to wear to the ball. They searched throughout the house and found sashes, scarves, buttons, and fabric that made a wonderful dress for Cinderella. When she finally finished her chores on the eve of the ball, the Mice gave her this dress. When she tried it on she looked gorgeous.

*Have the Mice come into the performing space and pretend to search around for things to make a dress. Once they've got them, they can begin to sew the imaginary dress together. It's always fun for them to cheer "hurray!" when they are finished making the dress. As you narrate, have Cinderella return to the performing space to try on the dress. She will love spinning around to show it off.*

But, when Cinderella came downstairs to show her new dress to her Stepmother and Stepsisters, they told her that the dress was made with all their belongings and ripped it apart until it looked like a rag. Cinderella ran outside and began to cry.

*Have Cinderella and the Mice walk downstairs (you may have to help them mime this). As their characters are called, the Stepmother and Stepsisters should return to the performing space. When they see Cinderella, each one should say "Hey, that's mine," and pretend to tear a piece of Cinderella's dress. Once her dress has been ripped, Cinderella should run to a far corner of the performing space to put on her sad face, and the Mice can follow her. The others can return to their seats. Always be sure to stress that when they are ripping her dress it's "pretend." There's no need for anyone to grab or hurt another child during the story.*

Just then a magical creature appeared and told Cinderella that she was her Fairy Godmother come to make her dreams come true. With the wave of a wand, she made an even more exquisite dress with glass slippers to match. She turned the Mice into horses and turned a pumpkin into a coach. The Fairy Godmother told Cinderella to make sure to be home by midnight, for that's when the spell would be broken. With gratitude, Cinderella left for the ball.

*As Cinderella is crying in the corner, call the Fairy Godmother to the performing space. It may be fun for her to dance or spin her way over to Cinderella. Cinderella should ask "Who are you?" and the Godmother can reply with "I am your Fairy Godmother." As you narrate, the Fairy Godmother can wave her wand to change Cinderella's dress and shoes, the Mice, and the pumpkin. She may like to accompany this by saying, "Bipadee-bopadee-boo," like in the Disney movie. Have the Fairy Godmother say to Cinderella, "You must be home by midnight," as Cinderella and the Horses leave for the ball. They can circle the performing space a couple of times until they get there. The Fairy Godmother can return to her seat.*

As soon as Cinderella arrived, the Prince noticed her, and the two danced with one another all night long. At midnight, Cinderella knew that the spell would break, and she ran from the Prince. He tried to stop her, but all he got was one of her glass slippers, which had fallen off as she was running away.

*Once the ball starts, call the Prince to the performing space. He can come over to Cinderella and say, "hello." After the introductions turn on some soft music and let everyone come into the space and begin dancing as though they were at the ball. When you stop the music, you may want to have everyone freeze to restore a bit of focus, or you can send all the children, except for Cinderella and the Prince, back to their seats. As you narrate the clock striking midnight, Cinderella should run away, and the Prince will chase her. She will run back to her seat, and the Prince will pick up the magic glass slipper.*

The next day, the Prince went to every house to find the girl whose foot fit the glass slipper. When he got to Cinderella's house, he found her.

*The Prince can go to everyone who is seated in the watching space and pretend to try the shoe on him or her. As he goes to each child, be sure to narrate that it doesn't fit. When he gets to Cinderella, the slipper will fit, and she can stand up and hold his hand (or if they are too shy to do that, they can simply stand together).*

They were married soon after. Cinderella and the Mice moved into the Prince's castle, and they lived happily ever after. The end.

Everyone stand up and take a big giant bow.

## FOLLOW-UP ACTIVITIES

### Being Nice to Others.
In this story, the Evil Stepmother and Evil Stepsisters do things to Cinderella that are not nice. Discuss this with your students and have them give you some examples of the mean things that they do to her. Talk about why it's important to be nice to other people.

Call each child up to the performing space. Ask how he or she could be nice to Cinderella if Cinderella were his or her sister. These answers may range from sharing a toy to telling her she looks pretty in her dress. The important thing to stress to the children is that if they are nice to others, others will be nice to them.

### Responsibilities and Chores.
Cinderella has many chores to do. Many people have to do some chore or another when they are at home. Talk to your students about the chores that Cinderella had to do in this story. Introduce the word *responsibility*. A simple definition is that a responsibility is something that a person is in charge of. Have the students repeat the word a couple of times to get the feel of it on their tongues. Give some examples of responsibilities that your students may have at home. Some examples can be making their bed, putting their shirts on by themselves, brushing their teeth, cleaning up their toys.

Call each child to the performing space and give that student a responsibility to act out silently. As they act it out, the other students will try to guess what task the student is performing. Let each child have a chance to do this activity. As you continue to use the word *responsibility*, the students will learn its sound and will begin to understand what it means.

### A Little Bit of Creativity.
Cinderella got to wear two beautiful dresses. Can you make something beautiful too? Discuss some of the things that may have made Cinderella's dress beautiful. Did it have nice colors? Was it sparkly? Were there pretty patterns on it? Ask your students to think of some other things that they find beautiful.

Sit in a circle. Explain to your students that you have an imaginary piece of clay in your hands, and that you are going to make something with it that you think is beautiful. When you have finished, tell them what you made and describe it. Then pass it to the student on your right or left and have them make something that they think is beautiful. It might be a butterfly, or it might be a fire truck. It doesn't matter as long as that student has made the decision by him- or herself. Once the student finishes, have him or her tell everyone what it is. Continue to pass the imaginary clay around the circle until everyone has had a chance.

# UNIT 4
# Adventure Stories

Adventure stories are great for imagination expansion and are a way to encourage your class to do things together as a group. In this section, your students will be traveling to a myriad of different places, from Mars to aquariums, from bakeries to beaches. Each adventure is designed to teach your students the function of the destination as well as to indulge their fantasies about each place.

There are rarely specific roles to be filled in adventure stories. The children will explore the imaginary circumstances as themselves. However, you may often have multiple roles to play throughout each journey that introduce the students to the many facets of each place.

The lessons in this unit are especially useful for a group of younger students (two-year-olds to early threes). The stories are not as structured as the ones in the previous section. Your younger students will have a bit more freedom to explore, rather than having to sit in their seats for extended periods of time, and your older students will still find these stories stimulating and fun. So get ready for the journey and have a great time.

# Trip to Space

## OBJECTIVES

- To expand the imagination through exploration

- To learn about outer space, and to play with students' perceptions of it

## STORY SYNOPSIS

A bunch of kids decided to take a trip to space. So they built themselves a spaceship, got in, and took off for outer space. As they were leaving Earth, they came to the clouds. They decided to land there and explore. They got out, felt how soft the clouds were, and jumped around like the clouds were trampolines. Next, the kids went to the moon. When they got out, they found out that they were lighter, and they started jumping and floating around. Next, the kids went to the sun. They got out and started to burn their feet. They had to run back into their spaceship because it was too hot on the sun. Next the kids went to the stars. The stars were bright but very far away from each other. Because the stars are as hot as the sun, they had to jump around from star to star as if they were jumping from rock to rock in a stream. As they jumped, the kids sang, "Twinkle, Twinkle Little Star." Finally they decided to go to a planet: Mars. On Mars, they saw a Martian. Everyone was very scared at first because he looked so different. But once the Martian came over to give the kids a hug, they knew everything was all right. When it was time to go home, they jumped back into the spaceship one last time and went back to Earth. They went to the playground where they had been playing, and they decided that they would definitely like to go to space again someday soon.

## NARRATOR

Once upon a time a bunch of kids were playing outside when all of a sudden, _____ said, "I have an idea. Let's go to space." The rest of the children thought that this was a great idea and they all yelled, "Yeah!"

*Encourage all the students to come into the performing space and pretend to play outside. Some examples of things that they can pretend to do are swinging on swings, building in the sand, playing tag. In the blank space above, you many insert one of the children's names. This will automatically prompt that child to repeat the line after you. Make sure that the other children put on their excited faces and give you a superloud "Yeah!"*

So they decided to build a spaceship. They built and built and built. As they were building, they each painted a part of it their favorite color.

*Building the spaceship can be made as intricate or as simple as you choose. It's great to ask the children what they are adding to the spaceship as they build it. You may want to let them run to every part of the room to get these imaginary objects. Once the spaceship is finished, the painting should begin. As everyone paints the spaceship with imaginary paintbrushes, it's a great time to encourage a little individuality by asking each student what color he or she is painting the ship.*

Then they got in. They put on their seat belts, turned the key, pressed all the buttons, and counted down from ten until finally, they blasted off.

*Have everyone sit down inside the spaceship and follow your directions. You can make up sounds that accompany each of the steps (a click for the seat belt, a vroom for the key, and so on).*

As they were leaving Earth, the first things they came to were the clouds. They decided to land there and explore. They got out, felt how soft the clouds were, and jumped around like the clouds were trampolines.

*Lead the children in slowly getting out of the spaceship (this will create a sense of wonder as you begin to look around). Have them reach down and feel how soft the clouds are. Then let 'em loose to jump around for a while. As you get back into the spaceship to go to the next place, have them follow the same directions for take-off as you did before (continuity is very important to them). Repeat this step after every new exploration in this lesson.*

Next they went to the moon. When they got out, they found out that they were much lighter, and they started floating around.

*Help the students explore the first feeling of slowly bouncing off the ground. They will associate floating with flying. Encourage them to float around the moon. Try to get the students to jump in slow motion. It will never work, but it's fun and silly, and the children will get a kick out of trying it.*

Next they went to the sun. They got out and started to burn their feet. They had to run back into their spaceship because it was too hot on the sun.

*You can play with lots of sun apparel before you get out of the spaceship if you choose (putting on sunglasses, applying sunblock, and so on). As soon as they get out and start to walk around, help the children realize how hot it's. As their feet start to get hot, show them that they need to jump from foot to foot to keep from burning themselves. A little scream of "ooch, ooch, ouch" may help this along. When everyone gets back to the spaceship, you may want to have everyone put their feet in some ice water to make them feel better.*

Next they went to the stars. The stars were bright, but very far away from each other. Because the stars are as hot as the sun, they had to jump around from star to star as if they were jumping from rock to rock in a stream. As they jumped, the kids sang, "Twinkle, Twinkle Little Star."

*Have your students jump from one foot to the other with big strides, as though they are visiting all the stars. This plays into their perception of stars being small, the way they see them in the sky. Singing "Twinkle, Twinkle Little Star" is an amusing way to move through this activity.*

Finally, they decided to go to a planet: Mars. On Mars, they saw a Martian. Everyone was very scared at first, because he looked so different. But once the Martian came over to give them a hug, they knew everything would be all right.

*Encourage your students to explore Mars a little bit before you introduce the Martian. They can pick up space rocks and climb a Martian mountain. It will work best if you become the Martian so that all the children can still participate in the exploration. Have the students put on their scared faces when they see you — they can even run to a corner and huddle together. As you walk closer to them and finally give them a big group hug, it's fun to have the children give a big sigh of relief.*

When it was time to go home, they jumped back into the spaceship one last time and went back down to Earth.

*Hop into the spaceship one final time and follow the take-off procedures that you have been doing throughout this lesson. Have the students say good-bye to each of the places you visited as you pass them on the way back down to Earth. It will provide a nice closure to your lesson. When you land on Earth, you may want to let each student off the spaceship one by one, calling each child's name as a signal to return to his or her seat.*

They went to the playground where they had been playing, and they decided that they would definitely like to go to space again someday soon. The end.

Everyone stand up and take a big giant bow.

## FOLLOW-UP ACTIVITIES

### What Do You Like About Space?
You have just visited a number of places in space with your students. Some of these may have been new to them, and they may know of others that you didn't cover on this trip (black holes, the rest of the planets, comets). Discuss what other things exist in space. Their knowledge will vary depending on the age group and the curriculum at your school. However, most preschool children can identify at least one thing that belongs in space. Encourage them to do so.

Call each student up to the performing space. Ask the child to describe his or her favorite thing about space. Ask the student why he or she likes that particular aspect of space. This exercise is designed to get the students talking about the things that interest them and to encourage them to stand in front of the class and speak.

## What Are the Clouds Really Like? In this story, everyone jumped up and down on the clouds as though they were trampolines. Can people really do that on a cloud? Discuss with your students what clouds are really like. Make a point of reminding them that in real life we can't really jump on the clouds, but we can feel the clouds every time it rains.

Have all the students spread out in the performing space and lie down flat. Explain to them that they are drops of water in a river. As the sun comes out, have them slowly get to their feet and float up into the air. Once they've floated for a while, have them all join hands to make a circle. Explain that this circle is like a cloud, where lots of tiny drops of water have come together. Then have them drop hands and float back down to the ground as rain. They should land in their original spot in the river. You can repeat this activity a couple of times, so that the students really begin to understand this process.

## What Does the Sun Do? In this story, the students walked on the sun and it burnt their feet. Can people really walk on the sun? Discuss how hot the sun actually is. Ask your students if they know how the sun helps us (keeps us warm, makes flowers grow).

Have each child find his or her own place in the performing space. Ask the children to sit on their knees and curl up into little balls. Count to twenty as they slowly grow into big beautiful flowers. As you do this, you may want to surprise them by telling them that the sun went behind a cloud for a while. Encourage their flowers to wilt until the sun comes out again. No wonder the sun needs to be so hot! It has to reach all these flowers to make them grow.

## Look Through a Telescope. The students just had a close look at space. But very few people ever really get to go in a spaceship. So how can people see what's up in space? Introduce the word *telescope*. Explain to your students how telescopes make everything that is far away look closer. Have them repeat the word after you a few times so that they can get it into their heads and get the feel for it on their tongues. Call each child up to the performing space, one by one. Have the child look in your imaginary telescope and ask what he or she sees.

# Day at the Beach

## OBJECTIVES

- To get students thinking about the different seasons
- To encourage creativity and individuality
- To continue working with the concept of cooperation

## STORY SYNOPSIS

There were some kids who wanted to go to the beach. So they packed their bags, got into their car, and left for the beach. The children decided that first they would take out their sand toys and build a giant sand castle. After a while, the kids got hot and decided to go swimming in the ocean. They jumped in and began to swim about. In the water, they looked at all the pretty fish and had swimming races. When it was time to get out, they sat on a blanket and ate lunch together. Then they got into the car again and headed back. Everyone was dropped off at home, and they all hoped that they could return to the beach again soon.

## NARRATOR

Once upon a time there were some kids who liked to play together. One day, _____ said, "I have an idea. Let's go to the beach." all the other children thought that this was a great idea, and they all cheered, "Yeah!"

*Have all the students come to the performing space and play together. Give them a few moments to interact with one another before moving on. Then, as you narrate, insert a student's name into the blank space. This will automatically prompt him or her to repeat the line after you. Make sure that all the students give a loud cheer of "Yeah!" after you narrate their doing so.*

So they got their things together, packed their bags, and got into their car.

*This is a great moment to encourage some individuality. As the students pack their bags, ask them what they are packing. Give each student a chance to tell you what's going into his or her bag. Once they've finished packing, point to where the car will be and have all the students sit down there as though they were getting in.*

Once in the car, they put on their seat belts, turned the key, pressed the buttons, and left for the beach. They drove around curves, down hills, and on bumpy roads. Finally they arrived.

*As you narrate the actions that help to start the car, have the students do them with you. You may want to incorporate sounds to go with the actions and have the students say those with you as well. As you are narrating the movements of the car, make sure to get your body into it. For example, when you go around curves, move your body from left to right. The students will see you doing this and will follow your example.*

When they got out of the car, they ran for the beach. The first thing they did was put on their sunblock to make sure they didn't get sunburned. Then they put on their swimming suits and their sunglasses.

*Let 'em loose as they hop out of the car. They can run to anywhere in the space. The wonderful thing about this lesson is the freedom it gives you and the students to use the entire space as your playing field. As you narrate, put on your sunblock with the students. This will prompt them to do the same. Likewise, put on your swimming suit and sunglasses. Kids love the idea of sunglasses and will enjoy the opportunity to don a pair.*

At last it was time to play. The children decided that first they would take out their sand toys and build a giant sand castle. They filled their buckets up with sand and turned them over again and again until they had many different towers. They built a moat and filled it up with water.

*If you wish, you may add to the narration by having a student say, "Let's build sand castles!" To do this, simply follow the format used at the beginning of the story. Let the children sit down where they are and build in the sand. It will help if you participate in the activity and assist with the castle building. If you see some students working together, you may want to let them continue for a moment.*

But, pretty soon, the kids got hot and decided to go swimming in the ocean. They jumped in and began to swim about. First they swam underwater and looked at all the pretty fish. They tried to catch the fish in their hands, but the fish were too fast for them and always got away. Next the children swam backward. And, after that, they had swimming races in the water. When it was time to get out, they grabbed their towels and dried themselves off.

*Again, you may want to give a student a line to say, like, "I'm hot. Let's go swimming!" As the students all jump into the ocean, give them a moment to play with their idea of water play before you continue on to the water activities. Then, as you narrate, the students will partake in the water activities with one another. Feel free to add others that you enjoy, like snorkeling, diving like dolphins, or your own personal favorites. As you narrate, have the students step out of the water and dry off.*

Then it was time for lunch. Everyone reached into their bags and pulled out their lunches. They sat down on blankets and towels and ate their yummy food. Some of the children even shared with one another.

*Sit down with the students to eat your picnic lunch. Encourage each student to tell the class what they are eating. As you narrate the sharing, let your students decide whether they will share with one another and allow their own dialogue to take over for a moment.*

Once they had finished eating, it was time to go home. They packed up their bags and made sure to take all their garbage with them. They got into the car again and headed back. Everyone was dropped off at home.

*The students should pack up their bags and throw away any trash that they've got. As you head back to the car, try to put it in the same spot it was before. Continuity is important to children of this age. Start the car as you did previously (complete with seat belts, ignition, button pushing, and whatever sounds you may have added). As you begin your drive home and drop the students off, it's nice to let each student have his or her own stop. A simple way to do this is to call each child's name, one by one. Have the other students say good-bye to the student and have that student return to his or her seat.*

And they all hoped that they could return to the beach again very soon. The end.

Everyone stand up and take a big giant bow.

## FOLLOW-UP ACTIVITIES

### Hot Fun in the Summer Time.
The students just took a trip to the beach, so the weather must have been hot in the story. What season is hotter than the others? What else can people do when it's hot? Discuss this with your students. You may need to review the seasons with them as you do this. The important thing is for the students to begin thinking of summer as a hot time. You can even refer to it as "hot summer" to get it into their heads.

Call each child to the performing space and ask him or her to tell you something that is fun to do when it's hot out. Your students may simply repeat their favorite activity from the lesson, or they might come up with new ones. It doesn't matter, as long as each child gets a chance to speak in front of the class and express an opinion of his or her own.

### Sand Castles.
Everyone worked together to make a giant sand castle in this story. If the students were building them by themselves, what would they look like? Talk to your students about the different things that could be added to a sand castle. Remind them that when they build something in the sand, it doesn't have to be a castle. It can be a house, a mountain, or anything else that they want to create.

Sit in a circle with the class. Explain to them that you have an imaginary bucket and a shovel in your hands and that there is a pile of sand in the center of the circle. Their job is to build their own sand sculpture. Go around the circle and give each student the sand toys, one at a time. Let them fill their bucket and sculpt for a moment. Once the student is finished, ask him to tell the class what he made. Once he has, let him knock it down and hand the sand toys to the next student. Give everyone a chance to create something and to show a bit more of his or her own individuality.

**The Cooperation Train.** In this story, everyone built a sand castle together. When people do things together, it's called cooperation. Discuss this idea with your students, introducing them to the word *cooperation*. Take a moment to ask them why cooperation is so important and what kinds of things they can do together (like playing with blocks or cleaning up). Remember to stress that things can go faster when people work on getting them done together.

It's time to make a Cooperation Train. Call your students to the space and explain to them that they are going to make a little pond in the sand. First, they must build a big hole. It will go faster if everyone does it together. So hand out imaginary shovels and begin to build. Then it's time to fill it with water, but the water is far away from the hole. So you will have to make a Cooperation Train. Have your students make a line stretching from the giant hole that they've just built to the ocean water. Then give the last student on line an imaginary bucket to fill with water. Once he's done, ask him to pass it to the next student, and so on, until the bucket finally reaches the student who is standing nearest to the hole. That student should dump the water into the hole and then pass the bucket back the way it came. Repeat this a number of times and try to increase their excitement and pace by relaying how much water is in the hole. Once it's full, let the students jump in and splash around in their new swimming hole. Make sure they give each other high-fives to thank one another for the hard work. And don't forget to congratulate them on their fine display of cooperation.

# Go on a Treasure Hunt

## OBJECTIVES

- To indulge the students' adventure fantasies

- To promote sharing with others

- To encourage individuality and creativity

## STORY SYNOPSIS

Some children found a treasure map and decided to go on a treasure hunt. First they drove to the forest on the map. They took five giant steps, crawled through a tunnel, jumped on rocks to get across a stream, climbed trees, and swung on vines. Then they hopped into a rowboat and rowed to the island on the treasure map. Once they were there, they followed the map until they found the treasure spot. They dug in the dirt until they found lots of treasure. But soon the children saw that pirates were coming, and the pirates surely wanted the treasure. The kids quickly followed their steps all the way back to the car and drove away, never to see the pirates again. When they got home, the kids agreed to meet the next day to show each other all their treasures. For now they went to bed, hoping that tomorrow would bring another adventure just like this one.

## NARRATOR

Once upon a time a bunch of really cool kids were sitting together and looking at some books. All of a sudden, _____ said, "Look what I found. A treasure map!" All the other kids were very excited, so they came closer to take a look. Sure enough, it was a treasure map. So, _____ said, "Let's go on a treasure hunt." The other kids thought that this was a great idea, and they all cheered, "Yeah!"

> *Call all your students to the performing space and let them sit for a moment, pretending to read books. Insert a child's name into the blank space. This will prompt him or her to repeat the line after you. As you narrate, the children should gather around and look at the treasure map. Insert a different child's name into the second blank space and let that child repeat the next line after you. Make sure that all your students give a big cheer of "Yeah!" as you narrate.*

They began to get ready for the trip. They packed their bags with all the important things: water, binoculars, shovels, and copies of the treasure map for each person.

*Have your students pack their imaginary backpacks. As you mention the particulars of what's going in, feel free to ask them if they think anything else should get packed. Let each child suggest something. Be sure to hand out a copy of the treasure map to each student; then it becomes real to them.*

Once they were all packed, they got into their car. Everybody put on their seat belts, turned the key, and pressed all the buttons. They drove a long way, over hills, around curves, and on bumpy roads, until finally they reached the forest.

*Point to where the car is going to be so the students will know where to sit down. (If you've already done a lesson with a car in it, try to use the same area of your performing space to place the car. Continuity is important to preschool children.) Have your students follow the directions as you narrate them, incorporating sounds if you wish. Make sure to use your body as you go up hills, around curves, and along bumpy roads. The children will see you doing it and follow your example.*

When they arrived, everyone got out of the car slowly. They looked at their treasure maps to find out where to go next. The map said that they needed to take five giant steps into the forest, so they did. Next the kids had to crawl through a tunnel and come out the other end. When they did that, they came out in a totally different part of the forest.

*As you narrate, have the students take slow steps to get out of the car. After the students look at their maps, they can follow your directions as to what comes next. They take five giant steps,. then they lie down on the ground and crawl across the space as though through a tunnel.*

They looked at their maps again. The map pointed them to a stream up ahead. The children had to cross the stream by jumping from rock to rock to make it across. Next the map said to climb up the trees nearest them, so they did. Once they were up there, they had to grab hold of the vines and swing from tree to tree until they could see the ocean. The children did this just like monkeys do. Then they slid down the vines all the way to the ground, and they saw the ocean right in front of them.

*Again, after looking at their maps, they will wait to hear what you say, and they will follow your directions. Have them jump from foot to foot as they cross the river. You may need to show them what it looks like to climb up the tree. Then grab onto the vines and run through the space as you swing on the vines. They will gladly follow you and have a great time doing it. When you slide down the vines, you can have the students simply slither to the floor.*

The kids looked at the map to see what was next and saw that they had to cross the ocean to get to a small island. Everyone took out their binoculars and looked through them to find the island. All at once, the children found the island and yelled, "Found it!"

*Have the students look at their maps once more and then reach into their bags for their binoculars. This is a great time to explain what binoculars do (they make things look closer), or you may wish to explain it before you even get started with your lesson. Choose whichever option feels right for you and your students. As the students look through their binoculars, they will repeat what they are supposed to say after you.*

So they got into a rowboat, put on their life jackets in case they fell in the water, and began to row. They rowed and rowed and then they saw a shark, so they rowed faster. Luckily they made it to the island without the shark. They pulled the boat to shore and took off their life jackets.

*This is a great place to add a little excitement to the story. Point to where the boat is going to be so that the students all go there together. Once they've begun to row, point the shark out to them. When they hear that they have to row faster, the group will become energized and will have a great time doing it. Be sure to have them take off their life jackets and pull the boat to shore.*

The children looked at their map for help. It directed them to walk in three big circles, jump up and down four times, and take two giant steps. They did this and then began to dig. After digging for just a moment, they each found a buried treasure.

*Once again, the students will do all these activities as you narrate them. Try to break it down, one at a time. Otherwise, they will not remember what comes next. Let each child dig his or her own separate hole so that each child can have his or her own treasure.*

But soon they saw some pirates coming. They knew they had to get back quickly. They took their treasures and put them in their bags. They didn't have time to talk about them now, but they would tell each other all about them later. They quickly got back into the rowboat, put on their life jackets, and rowed as fast as they could. When they got to shore, they climbed up the trees and swung on the vines. Then they jumped on the rocks to cross the stream. They crawled through the tunnel, took five giant steps, and were back at the car. As fast as they could, the children hopped into the car, put on their seat belts, turned the key, pressed the buttons, and sped away.

*Once the excitement of the chasing pirates sets in, you will be able to backtrack each activity as quickly as you like.*

As the kids were leaving, they could see that the pirates would never catch up to them. They drove back home feeling great about their trip. Each child was dropped off at home, and they promised each other that the next day they would tell each other what kind of treasure they had found.

*As you drive back home, drop each child off individually. You can easily do this by calling each child's name to indicate that he or she should return to his or her seat.*

For now, they went to bed, hoping that tomorrow would bring another adventure just like this one. The end.

Everyone stand up and take a big giant bow.

## FOLLOW-UP ACTIVITIES

The Buried Treasure. In this story, the students found buried treasure but didn't get a chance to share what they found. Now is their chance to do that. Call each child to the performing space and ask that student to tell the class what he or she found. Don't be surprised at some of the answers that you hear. They will range from Power Ranger toys to Barbie dolls to gold. Any answer is good as long as the students are speaking from their own imagination. Once each student has revealed his or her treasure, have the student take it out of his or her bag to show the others. Once the students have done that, they can return to their seats.

Sharing the Loot. Everyone has heard what all the other students found as their buried treasure. Would anyone like to share and have others share with them? Discuss this with your students. Talk to them about why it's important to share, and explain what people gain when they do share with friends. Stress that if a person shares with a friend, then the friend will usually share in return.

Sit in a circle with your students and tell them to bring their treasure along with them to the circle. Once everyone is seated, explain to the class that it's time to share. Go around the circle and ask each student to remind the others of what kind of treasure he or she got. Then ask your students, one at a time, if they would like to share with the others. Since they know it's the right thing to do, they will usually agree to share. Have that student hand out a piece of his or her treasure to the rest of the circle. Make sure that everyone thanks that student before moving on to the next person in the circle. Once everyone has had a chance to share his or her treasure with the rest of the class, remind them how nice it's to have lots of different kinds of treasure instead of just one kind. This is a result of their wonderful sharing efforts.

Where Does Your Treasure Map Point? In this story, everyone followed a treasure map through the forest, over an ocean, and onto an island. Talk to your students about all the different places they went in this story. Then explain to your students that a map doesn't only direct a person toward treasure. Some maps show how to get to other states or other countries.

Spread the students out in the space, giving each child his or her own place to sit down. Explain to them that they are each going to get a chance to make their own map to wherever they would like to go. Walk through the room and give each student his or her own piece of imaginary paper and crayons. Give them a few moments to draw their imaginary maps. When time is up, come together as a group, either in a circle or in seats. Ask each child where his or her map will take people. Let the student show his or her imaginary map to the rest of the class and allow the child to talk in as much detail about it as he or she likes. This activity is a great way for students both to let their imaginations take flight and to realize some of their fantasies about adventure and exploration. When everyone is finished, tell the class to take these maps and stick them in their pockets. They will come in handy on a day when they want to go on another imaginary exploration with the rest of their friends.

# Go on an African Safari

## OBJECTIVES

- To introduce students to Africa
- To familiarize students with different animals

## STORY SYNOPSIS

Some kids decided to take a trip to Africa to see the animals. They packed their bags and took an airplane to get there. Then their African safari began. First they saw elephants bathing in a river. A baby elephant wanted to play with the kids, so she offered them a ride on her back. And pretty soon all the elephants were giving the kids rides. Next the kids saw a herd of zebras. The kids tried to chase the zebras, but the zebras were running so fast that their stripes began to blur and look like tall grass. Next the kids saw some giraffes that were eating. They noticed that the baby giraffes couldn't reach their necks up high enough to grab the leaves. The children helped by climbing up onto the giraffes' backs, walking up their long necks, and grabbing leaves for them. Then they slid down the giraffe's necks like a slide. Finally, at the end of the day, the children rolled out their sleeping bags and slept under the stars. The next day they flew home. The children hoped they would get to travel to more places like this again very soon.

## NARRATOR

Once upon a time some kids were playing outside pretending to be jungle animals. All of a sudden, _____ said, "I have an idea. Let's go to a real jungle." Everyone thought that this was a great idea and said, "Yeah!" So they began to pack their bags. They put in all the important things for their African safari like sleeping bags, food, and binoculars.

> *Have all your students come to the performing space and let them pretend to be jungle animals for a few moments. Insert a student's name into the blank space in the story. That will prompt the student to repeat the line after you. Make sure that the rest of the children respond with a big "Yeah!" As you narrate, the students will begin to pack up their bags with the things that you have suggested. Feel free to let them suggest other things that they should take with them.*

When they were finished packing, the children had to get onto an airplane because Africa is far away. So everyone got onto the plane, found their seats, put on their seat belts, and waited for takeoff. As the plane took off, the kids looked out the windows to see all the beautiful things they were flying over on the way to Africa. They saw a huge ocean and many fields and mountains that looked far away.

*As you introduce the airplane, point to where it is so that the students know where to go. Once they've gotten on, they will follow your directions and fasten their seat belts. Let the students look out the imaginary windows as you narrate the takeoff. They may blurt out other things that they see through the windows. It means that their imaginations are with you every step of the way.*

Soon the plane landed, and the students took their bags and got off. It was time for their African safari to begin. They got into a car that would take them to see the animals and the jungle. They drove up hills and around curves, and finally the car stopped.

*As the plane lands, it might be fun to add a thumping noise to indicate the landing. The children will catch onto this and do it with their bodies. If you have used the car in other drama lessons, try to put it in the same spot in your performing space as you have in your other stories. This will create a feeling of continuity for your students, which is important to them. Get your body into the action as you narrate the hills and curves. The students will see you doing this and will follow your example.*

"The children slowly got out because they knew that they had to be careful not to scare any of the animals. They took out their binoculars and looked in them to see if they could find any animals in the distance. Soon, _____ said, "I see elephants!" and pointed to where they were. The children tiptoed over to where the elephants were and watched them for a moment. The elephants were taking a bath in a river.

*Make sure that your students take slow steps as they get out of the car. You may have to show them how to hold binoculars up to their eyes. Many children this age have never seen binoculars before, so they are learning about them for the first time. Insert a student's name into the blank space in the story again, and that will prompt the student to repeat the line after you. Let the children tiptoe to the watching spot. You many even want to have them crouch down as they try to stay out of sight. It's always fun to whisper this part to make it seem as though the elephants could hear you if you speak too loudly.*

All of a sudden, the elephants saw the children, and the children got scared. They knew that elephants are much bigger than they are, and the kids didn't want to upset the elephants. But a baby elephant walked right over to the children and offered them a ride on her back. Pretty soon the other elephants could see that the kids didn't want to hurt them, and they all came and gave the kids rides on their backs. After the ride, the children patted the elephants and said good-bye and then continued on their way.

*Make sure that your students put on their scared faces when they hear that the elephants have seen them. You may want to act as the baby elephant or you may want to have the students continue to imagine the animals. Either way is fine, as long as the students don't actually climb onto your back. Let the children climb onto the backs of the pretend elephants and ride around the space with their legs straddled wide to fit over the animal's enormous back. As you narrate, the children will pat the backs of their new friends and say good-bye to them.*

Next, _____ said, "I see some zebras!" and pointed to where the zebras were. Again, the kids tiptoed over to the zebras so that they wouldn't scare them. But the zebras heard them coming and began to run away. Soon the kids couldn't even see them anymore. The stripes on the zebras were beginning to look like tall grass. And soon they were gone.

*Insert a student's name into the blank space and have him or her say the next line. Your students will tiptoe to the space that you have pointed to. It may be fun for you to act as a zebra that is running away throughout the space. Be warned that this will most likely cause your students to chase after you for a moment, but a good chase scene is always fun and will simply add a little more excitement to your story.*

All of a sudden, a group of giraffes came galloping through the field. They stopped to eat, but the kids noticed that the baby giraffes couldn't reach their necks high enough to get the leaves off the trees. So they climbed up onto the baby giraffes and walked all the way up their long necks. At the very top, the kids were able to reach high enough to get the leaves, and they brought some back down to the giraffes. The giraffes were very happy. When it was time for the giraffes to go, the kids waved good-bye to them as they galloped away.

*Point to where the giraffes are galloping. As you narrate, have the students climb up onto the giraffes and walk up their necks. It will help if you do it as well and show them that they will need to balance as though they were on a balance beam. Once they have grabbed some leaves, they can spend a moment with their new friends. Again, you may want to play a giraffe at this point. The students will enjoy trying to feed leaves to you. As you narrate, the children will wave good-bye to the giraffes. If you have been playing a giraffe, it might be helpful for you to gallop around the space for a moment to indicate that, as a giraffe, you are leaving.*

It began to get dark and it was getting to be time for bed. So, the kids took out their sleeping bags and got inside them. They lay down and looked up at the stars for a bit before they went to sleep.

*Have the students roll out their sleeping bags and climb into them. Once they lie down, let them look up at the sky for a moment and then go to sleep.*

They next morning they packed up their sleeping bags, ate some breakfast, and got back into their car. They drove to the airport and then got onto the airplane. They flew all the way back home, and everyone was dropped off at his or her house. That night when they went to sleep, the kids remembered all the wonderful things that they did and saw in Africa.

*Let the students pack up their bags and eat some of their pretend food. Then they should get back into the car in the same place that it was located at the beginning of the story. The same goes for the placement of the airplane. To drop everyone off at home, simply call each student by name. When that student hears his or her name, it will be the signal to return to their seats.*

And they hoped that they would get to visit new places like that again very soon. The end.

Everyone stand up and take a big giant bow.

## FOLLOW-UP ACTIVITIES

### Where Would You Like to Visit? In this story, the students went to another continent called Africa. Have they ever been to another continent before? Where would they like to go? Discuss the distance between Africa and home. In the story, the students had to take an airplane to get to Africa. Ask if anyone has ever taken an airplane before. Encourage your students to talk about places that they have been, even if it was not in an airplane. Their answers may be as simple as going to Grandma's or to a summer home. The idea is to get your students thinking about places outside their own town.

Call each student up to the performing space. Ask that student where he or she would like to visit. Let the child know that it can be anywhere he or she desires. Disneyland is just as acceptable as the moon. Once the students have given you their answer, congratulate them for their creativity and individuality.

### Looking Through Binoculars. In this story, the students had to look through binoculars to see some of the animals. What are binoculars? Discuss this with your students. A simple explanation for what binoculars do is that they make things look closer. Have the students repeat the word after you a couple of times.

Have each student come to the performing space and look through imaginary binoculars. Ask them to tell you one thing that they can see as they are looking through the lenses. Encourage them to tell the rest of the class about this object before they sit down. This activity will not only introduce this new word to them, but it will also help your students become familiar with how binoculars work.

### Our Favorite African Animals. The students saw elephants, zebras, and giraffes in the story. What other animals live in Africa? Ask your students to give you examples of other animals that may live in Africa. They may know some, and others you may have to tell them about. Some animals to include in this activity are rhinos, monkeys, snakes, lions, hippos, leopards, and cheetahs.

Sit in a circle with your students. Go around the circle and ask each student to tell you what his or her favorite African animal is. Then ask that child to become that animal, and let him or her gallop around the circle for the class. Most of your students will be glad to romp about. If a child does not want to stand up and become the animal, you can encourage other students to do it with him or her, or you can let the student stay seated and simply help him or her make the sound of that animal.

Once everyone has had a chance, let the animals loose for a few moments. Tell them that they are in Africa again and that they can all be their favorite African animals. Remind them that the animals need to get along if they are going to live together in the same space. This will help to ensure that the lions, cheetahs, and other aggressors do not spend the entire time trying to fight with one another. After you've let them explore this environment for a few minutes, call the animals back to the circle. Have the students take off their animal suits and return to being themselves.

# A Trip to the Pet Store

## OBJECTIVES

- To teach students responsibility

- To indulge the students' fantasies about pets

## ROLES FOR STUDENTS TO CHOOSE FROM

In addition to playing themselves in this story, your students will also have the chance to play an animal in the pet store. Some roles to let them choose from include:

Dog    Cat    Bird    Fish    Rabbit    Snake

## STORY SYNOPSIS

The children decided to go to a pet store. While they were there, they watched the fish as they were fed, saw the birds fly around their cages, threw balls for the puppies, gave carrots to the bunnies, watched the snakes slither around, and saw the cats cleaning themselves and playing. Then each child got to choose their own animal to take home as a pet. As they left the pet store with their new pets, the children knew that this pet would be a very good friend for a long time to come.

## NARRATOR

Once upon a time some kids were looking at pictures of animals. They liked looking at the animals so _____ said, "Let's see some real animals. Let's go to a pet store!" All the other kids thought that this was a great idea and they all yelled, "Yeah!"

> *Call all the children to the performing space and let them sit down to look at their pretend books for a moment. Insert a student's name into the blank space in the story. This will prompt that child to repeat the line after you. The rest of the students should repeat the "yeah!" after you and put on their excited faces.*

So they ran out to their car, got in, and got ready to go. They buckled their seat belts, turned the key, pressed all the buttons, and drove off. They had to go around some curves to get there, but once they were there, they parked the car and got out.

*If you have used the car in previous lessons, be sure to place it in the same spot of the performing space for continuity's sake. To get your car going, your students will follow the directions you narrate for them.*

They walked into the pet store to see the animals. First they looked in the fish tanks and saw many beautiful fish. While they were watching the fish, they saw a caretaker come to feed them. The caretaker carefully sprinkled a bit of food into each tank, and the fish swam up to the top to eat their lunch.

*Lead your students to an outer edge of the performing space where they can watch the fish in their tanks. Then, as you introduce the fish, have the students who are playing the fish swim into the center of the performing space. You will act as the caretaker as you sprinkle the fish food around. Make sure your fish swim up to the top to get the food. The fish should return to being students as you finish this section of the story.*

Next the kids went over to the bird cages. The birds were sitting on their perches. Some were eating apples and others were pecking at the bird food that the caretaker had left for them. When the birds saw the children, they started flying around the cage to show off.

*Lead your students to a new area of the performing space. As you introduce the birds, let the students who are playing them fly into the center of the space. They will do all the actions you narrate for them. The birds should go back to playing themselves as you finish this section and join the rest of the children.*

Next the children went to see the puppy dogs. Some of the puppies were taking naps, and some of them were chasing their tails. The caretaker gave the kids some balls to throw to the dogs. The dogs caught the balls in their mouths and began to play with each other. They barked and wagged their tails to let the kids know how much they liked them.

*Lead your students to yet another area of the performing space. As you introduce the puppies, the children playing the dogs can crawl into the center of the performing space. As the caretaker, you can give the other students balls to throw to the dogs. Give the dogs a few moments to really romp about. The students playing dogs will return to themselves as you finish this section.*

Next the kids went to look at the rabbits. They were also in cages, but they could still hop around. They were fluffy and soft, and the caretaker let the children pet the bunnies for a moment. But the children had to be gentle so the rabbits wouldn't get scared. They fed the rabbits some carrots and moved on.

*Lead your students to a new area in the space. Your bunnies should hop into the center of the performing space as you introduce them. Give them a moment to hop around. Then, as you narrate, allow the other students to come over and pet the bunnies. Make sure to supervise that this is done gently. As the caretaker, you can give the students some pretend carrots for them to feed to the bunnies. The bunnies can go back to playing children again once this section is finished.*

Next the children went to see the snakes. Most of the snakes were coiled up and sleeping, but some of them were slithering around. Some people are afraid of snakes and don't even like to look at them in cages, so the snakes were happy when children came over. They hissed and slithered to show the kids how happy they were that they had come for a visit.

*Lead your students to another area of the space. Let the snakes slither into the center of the performing space and move around for a moment, following your directions as you narrate. Some of your students may be afraid of snakes. You can use this time to let them feel safe with the pretend snakes, or you can let them turn away so they don't have to see them. Assess how extreme the fear is before making your decision, and be sure not to force anyone into a situation where he or she feels uncomfortable. Once the section is finished, the snakes should turn back into children.*

Finally, the children went to visit the kitty cats. The cats were very busy cleaning themselves and playing with toys. They meowed and purred when they saw the kids watching them.

*Lead the students to one final area of the space to watch the cats. Let the cats crawl into the center of the performing space as they follow your narration. It may be fun to let the cats come over to the other students when they see them and let the other students pet them for a bit. Once again, the cats should turn back into children at the end of this section.*

Once the children had seen all the animals, it was time to choose one that they could each take home. So each child chose their pet and brought it to the checkout counter. They paid for their new animal, made sure to buy some pet food, and met back at the car.

*The children should all be themselves for the remainder of the story. Let them walk throughout the space and choose one animal to take home. You can be the cashier. Encourage your students to come to you and pay for their new pet and their pet's food. Then make sure your students return to the car (in the same place it was in the beginning of the story).*

They got back into their car, buckled their seat belts (and their pet's seat belt), turned the key, pressed all the buttons, and drove away from the pet store. On the way home, the children made sure to pet their new animals to show them how much they loved them. At last, each child was dropped off at home. They took their new pets with them and brought them into their houses.

*Have your students follow your narration while starting the car. It's fun to have them buckle their pet's seat belt as well. To drop each child off, simply call his or her name. This will prompt them to return to their seats (with their pet, of course).*

The children knew that they had just brought home an animal that was going to be a very good friend for a long time. And they were happy that they had made a trip to the pet store today. The end.

Everyone stand up and take a big giant bow.

## FOLLOW-UP ACTIVITIES

**What is Your Pet?** In this story, all the students got new pets. Find out what everyone took home with them. You may want to begin this activity by asking the students whether any of them have a real pet at home. Encourage them to take turns telling everyone what kind of pet they have and what their animal's name is.

Now find out about the pretend pets from today's story. Call each child to the performing space. Ask each student what kind of animal he or she bought on the pretend trip to the pet store. Be sure to find out what the child will name the pet. This gives the children a chance to live out some of their fantasies about having an animal, and it's a great way to encourage them to speak in front of their peers.

**A New Responsibility.** Having a pet is a big responsibility. The students will have to take good care of their new friends. Introduce the word *responsibility* to your students. An easy definition for your students to understand is that a responsibility is something that they are in charge of. Have them repeat the word after you a few times. Then discuss some examples of responsibilities that they might have in real life, for instance, making their bed, putting on their clothes in the morning, brushing their teeth. Next take a moment to discuss the responsibilities that come along with owning a pet. You can revisit your earlier discussion about students who have pets at home. Ask these students about some of the responsibilities involved in having a pet, like walking them, feeding them, and giving them baths.

Sit in a circle with your students, and tell them to bring their new pet to the circle as well. Go around the circle and ask each student to tell you one new responsibility he or she will have with this new pet. Once the student has told you, let that child stand up with his or her animal and perform this activity — for example, the child could walk his or her dog around the circle. Make sure that each student has a chance. Once everyone has had a turn, encourage your students to give their pet a treat for being so good during this lesson.

# Deep-Sea Dive

## OBJECTIVES

- To teach students about underwater life
- To explore the imagination through storytelling

## STORY SYNOPSIS

A group of kids took a boat out to the ocean to go on a deep-sea dive. They jumped into the water. They saw beautiful fish that they tried to touch, swam with dolphins, and rode on the backs of whales. Then they swam deeper to the ocean floor. There they saw lobsters that snapped their claws when the children tried to pet them and snails that peeked out of their shells when the children held them in their hands. As the children swam back to the surface, they said good-bye to all their new friends, and then they took the boat back to school. Now every time they look in the fish tank at school, the children think of their own deep-sea adventure.

## NARRATOR

Once upon a time a group of kids were at school looking at the fish tank. They were very interested in the fish inside and enjoyed watching them swim around. All of a sudden, _____ said, "I have an idea. Let's go to the ocean and see bigger fish." The other kids thought that this was a great idea and they all cheered, "Yeah!"

*Have all your students come into the performing space and look at the make-believe fish tank. Let them observe for a moment. Some of the students may begin to call out things that they see in the fish tank. It means that your students are turning their imaginations over to the world of the story. Insert a student's name into the blank space in the narration. This will prompt that child to repeat the line after you. As always, make sure that the rest of the students reply with a loud "yeah!" as they put on their excited faces.*

The kids all ran over to their boat. Before getting in, they put on their life jackets. Then they climbed into the boat and met the captain. The captain let the kids help him start the motorboat that would take them out into the ocean. Each of the children was told to start the engine, press some buttons, and pull up the anchor. The boat sped off. They sailed out to the middle of the ocean where they would begin their deep-sea dive.

*Point to where the boat will be so that your students know where to go. You may have to demon-strate putting on the life jacket or do it with your students, as this is probably something most have them have never done. They will watch you do it and follow your example. You may want to play the captain and shake each of the children's hands as they get onto the boat, or you can let him be imaginary; either option will work. The students will follow your directions for starting the boat. It's always fun to add some noises, such as the engine starting and the buttons beeping.*

Once they were out in the ocean, the children took off their life jackets and put on their sea masks and their flippers. They counted to three, and all the children jumped into the water with a big splash.

*As you narrate, the students will remove their life jackets and put on their diving gear. Simply count to three and all the children will jump in the air as though they were diving into the ocean.*

As soon as they were in the water, they could see lots of little fish swimming around them. The kids reached their arms out and tried to grab the pretty fish, but fish swim very fast and they kept swimming away. So the children decided to swim deeper to see some different animals.

*Let the children pretend to swim around for a moment. They will follow your narration and reach out to try and catch the fish. You may want to ask them to call out some colors that they see on the different fish.*

Then they saw dolphins. The dolphins were swimming through the water very fast so the chil-dren followed them. Every now and then, the dolphins would swim up to the top and jump out of the water. The children followed.

*Have your students swim around with the dolphins for a few moments. They will jump out of the water every time you narrate that the dolphins do it. Feel free to let them repeat this a cou-ple of times.*

Next the kids saw some humongous whales swimming their way. As the whales swam by, the children hopped on their backs and swam through the water with them. The whales also came up to the top of the water every now and then, and the children went with them. Then the chil-dren hopped off of the whales backs and waved good-bye to them as the whales swam away.

*The students should raise one leg and throw it over the back of an imaginary whale. Let them ride around like this for a moment as they enjoy the fantasy. Then, as you narrate, they will hop off and wave good-bye to their new friends.*

Next the children decided to swim deeper into the ocean to explore what was near the ocean floor. Once they had reached the bottom, they saw different kinds of animals than they had seen before. There were lobsters crawling around, and the children crawled around with them.

But when the kids tried to pet the lobsters, the lobsters snapped their claws at them. So the children decided to leave them alone.

*The children will swim toward the floor as you narrate their descent. Once they see the lobsters, encourage them to crawl around like these creatures. Make sure that when they stick their hands out to pet the lobsters, they pull them back quickly as though the lobsters snapped at them. Your students will enjoy this little game, so feel free to let them try it a couple of times.*

They also saw snails hiding in the sand of the ocean floor. They carefully picked up the snails in their hands and waited for the snails to peek their heads out from their protective shells. When they did, the kids talked to the snails for a moment and found out each snail's name. They put the snails back down and swam on.

*Have your students slowly pick up the snails and hold them in their hands. You may want to have each student tell the rest of the class what his or her snail's name is. This will encourage some creativity and individuality, not to mention fun.*

It was time to swim back up to the boat. The children slowly began to swim back up to the top, saying good-bye to their new friends along the way. Once they got to the surface, they used the ladder to climb back into the boat. The children dried themselves off, put on their life jackets, sat down, and got ready for the boat to head back to shore. They helped start the engine, press the buttons, and pull up the anchor.

*As they swim back up to the top, remind them of the different animals that they saw on their adventure so that they can say good-bye to each of these creatures. As you narrate, the students should climb up the ladder, get back into the boat, dry off, and put their life jackets on. They will follow your directions again as to how to start the boat.*

As the boat got to shore, the kids all said good-bye to their captain and went back into their schoolroom. When they went to look at their fish tank again, the children remembered what it was like to be able to swim around like those fish.

*As your students get off the boat, they should return to the place where the fish tank was and look inside it again. Give them a moment to observe.*

And they hoped that they could go on another deep-sea adventure again very soon. The end.

Everyone stand up and take a big giant bow.

## FOLLOW-UP ACTIVITIES

**What Is Your Favorite Ocean Animal?** In this story, the students saw dolphins, whales, lobsters, and snails. What other animals live in the ocean? Discuss this with your students. They may be able to come up with a number of different examples, or you may have to help them. Some animals to include are sharks, eels, sea turtles, octopuses, and sea horses.

Call each child up to the performing space. Ask that student to tell the class what his or her favorite sea animal is. Once he or she has, let the student swim around the performing space like that animal. This activity will encourage your students to make their own decisions and to speak aloud in front of their peers.

**A Submarine Ride.** In the story, the students swam through the ocean. What are some other ways to travel underwater? Pose this question to your students. Let them brainstorm for a bit as they try to come up with ideas. If the idea of a submarine does not come up, introduce it to them. Have them repeat the word after you a few times to get the feel of it on their tongues.

It's time to take a submarine ride. Call all your students to the performing space and tell them that they are going to build their own submarine. Let them run throughout the space to find the building pieces. As they assemble the submarine, make sure that the students include windows and a periscope to look through. This is a great time to let them know that a periscope helps a person see what's happening on top of the water, above the submarine. Once they've finished building the submarine, have the students climb in. Seat them in two rows, back to back (like in musical chairs). This will create the illusion that they are looking out the windows that are on either side of the submarine. As they travel through the water, encourage your students to look out the windows and call out the different kinds of underwater life that they see. When they are finished with their submarine ride, the students should climb out and return to their seats. Congratulate them on their hard work in making the submarine.

**How Do Sea Animals Breathe.** In the story, the dolphins and whales kept coming up to the top of the water. Why did they do this? Pose this question to your students. See if they can come up with the answer themselves. If not, help them to realize that these animals were coming up to the surface to breathe. Then discuss how fish breathe water through their gills to get oxygen.

Have all your students come to the performing space. Call out different kinds of ocean life one by one and have your students swim around and breathe like these creatures. For example, as they swim like whales, they should come up to the top and take a big gulp of air before swimming on. When they are swimming like eels, they can use their hands as gills and filter the water. You may need to remind them how each animal takes in oxygen. The most important thing is that they are learning how each of these underwater creatures lives and breathes. Finish the activity by having the students walk around as children taking deep breaths for themselves.

# Trip to the Bakery

## OBJECTIVES

- To educate students about how baked goods are made

- To encourage creativity and individuality

- To explore individual likes and dislikes

During this lesson, your students will be learning how things are made in a bakery, and they will be making cookies and pies. To do this, they will use an imaginary oven. Therefore you may want to take a moment before you begin your lesson to discuss some basic oven safety. Stress that what they do in drama class is pretend, but at home a real oven can be hot and dangerous. You don't want your students to think that this lesson now gives them the authority to use their oven at home without an adult present.

## STORY SYNOPSIS

A group of kids followed their noses toward the good smells of a bakery. They went inside and learned all about how cookies, breads and pies are made. First, they made the cookies by putting flour, butter, eggs, and sugar into a giant bowl. They hopped into the giant bowl and ran in circles to mix the ingredients together. Then they rolled out the dough by jumping on it, they cut out cookie shapes, and they put the cookies in the oven to bake. Next they made pies. They filled up the piecrusts with things like apples and peaches. One of the children suggested that they all hop in and make a Kid Pie. But once they realized that they would have to bake in the hot oven, they quickly hopped out and filled it with chocolate instead. When the pies and cookies were finished, the kids ate them up and thanked their new friends, the bakers. Then they went home, lay down in the grass, and dreamt of bakeries, pies, and good things to eat.

## NARRATOR

Once upon a time some kids were playing outside with each other. They were running around having a good time, when suddenly they all stopped! The children sniffed and smelled something so good that they started to get hungry. So, _____ said, "Let's go find out where that good smell is coming from." Since the other kids were getting hungry too, they all gladly yelled, "Yeah!," and they began to search for the scent.

*Have all the children come into the performing space and run around together for a moment as though they were playing a game. When you announce that they all stopped, the students will freeze in their tracks and wait for what's next. They should all sniff big breaths as you narrate them doing so. You may want to encourage the children to rub their stomachs to show that they're hungry. Insert one of the student's names into the blank space in the story. This will prompt that child to repeat the line after you. As always, make sure the rest of the students repeat "yeah!"*

They walked around sniffing and smelling, following their noses. They had to climb up hills and look both ways so that they could cross streets, but they kept on walking. After turning a corner, all the children stopped. They looked straight ahead and saw the building where the good smell was coming from. It was a bakery, where bakers make breads, pies, and cakes. The children decided to go in and find out how these yummy things get made.

*You can have the students follow you around the room or allow them to explore on their own. Just remember to make sure that they are sniffing and searching for that good smell. As you narrate, the students will climb pretend hills and look both ways before crossing the pretend street. The children stop as the narration dictates. Some may even call out, "There it's!" They are giving over their imaginations to the world of the story.*

They tiptoed toward the back door and opened it. There they saw an amazing sight: fifty people making breads and pies. The children thought that this was their lucky day, and they all began to cheer "Hooray!" because they thought that all this food was for them to eat. So they decided to find out how it all got made.

*Point to where the bakery door will be so that your students know where to tiptoe toward. You may want to start them off with some "oohs" and "aahs," as they look into the bakery for the first time. They will gladly echo "hooray!" as you narrate it in the story.*

First the children walked over to where the dough got made, and they decided to help. They put on their aprons and their baker's hats, washed their hands, and got to work. The children poured big bags of flour and sugar into big bowls full of eggs and butter.

*You may need to put on an apron and baker's hat too, so that the students can follow your example. Point to a section of the room where the imaginary sinks are located so that your students can all wash their hands. It's helpful to place your giant bowl in the center of the space. This will make it accessible to all the students, and it will make this activity the focus of the story for the time being. As you narrate, have your students pour enormous bags of all the ingredients. Since the bags are so big, you may want to encourage the students to help one another pour them. Add as many other ingredients as you like, such as chocolate chips or peanuts. Take suggestions from the children.*

Then it was time to mix it all in a huge bowl. In fact, the bowl was so big that all the kids decided to hop inside. They worked together and walked in a circle, round and around. This way, they helped to stir all the ingredients.

*This is fun to do with your students. Hop into the pretend bowl with them. Make sure that every-one is walking in the same direction while you stir the ingredients together. Shuffling feet may work well in mixing it all up.*

When this was done, the dough needed to be rolled out. Many of the bakers were doing this with rolling pins, so the children all got rolling pins and began to roll out the dough, too. This took a long time, and the kids had a better idea. They put their rolling pins down and began to jump up and down on the dough to flatten it out.

*Let the children run to any place in the room to get their own rolling pin. Then show them how to roll dough. Once you've given this a try, the children will follow your narration, dropping the rolling pins and jumping around the room. It's fun and silly, and your students will love it.*

Next the dough needed to be cut into cookie shapes and put into the oven. So the children cut out cookies, put them in a pan, and slid them into the oven. Then they took some more batter and poured it into a big pan to make bread. They put this in the oven, too.

*You can make the cookie cutting as intricate or as simple as you and your students wish. Give them pretend cookie cutters, telling them what shapes you've given them, and show them how to press them into the giant sheet of dough. Allow the students to continue doing this for a few moments. It will empower them to do this pressing on their own. Once they've finished, show the students where the pan is, and they will bring the cookies over to it and put them on top. Then point to where the pretend oven is, and let them open it and put the cookies inside. You can fol-low the same basic steps to make the bread as well, having them pour the batter into a pan and bringing it to the oven together.*

Last, they took some more dough and put it into a pan to make a pie. They filled the pie with lots of tasty ingredients. Some pies had apples in them, and some had peaches. All the kids jumped into one of the pies and said, "Let's make a Kid Pie!" But _____ said, "No, then we'll have to bake in the oven and that's too hot." The children agreed and hopped out. They put chocolate into the pie instead and put it in the oven too.

*Help your students take the dough and place it into some pie dishes to make the crusts. Then, as you narrate, they will fill up these pie dishes with apples and peaches or whatever else your students may suggest. As you narrate, your students will all jump inside one of the pies and re-peat their lines after you. Insert another student's name into the blank space in the story. This will prompt that student to repeat the next line after you. Have fun pouring in the chocolate. You can encourage the children to lick their fingers when they're done if you think it would be ap-propriate.*

While they were waiting for the pies to bake, the kids took off their aprons and washed their hands. Then, after some time, the kids went over to the ovens, carefully opened the oven door, and took out the breads, cookies, and pies.

*As you narrate, your students will take off their imaginary aprons and baker's hats. Then they should return to the place where the sinks are located and wash their hands. They will follow your directions as they carefully open the oven door and take out all the baked goods.*

They smelled so good that the children just had to sit down and try them out right then. They tried all the cookies, pies, and breads. Some of them were very yummy and some of them were not. They gulped down a big glass of milk to finish it off and then it was time to go.

*Make sure that your students put on their hungry faces as they smell and see the baked goods for the first time. Sit in a circle as everyone tastes everything. Encourage your students to talk about which things they are enjoying and which ones they don't like. They will hear your instructions and gulp down a glass of milk.*

The children said good-bye to all the bakers, said thank you for letting them help, and walked out the door. They had to look both ways and cross some streets and go over some hills on the way home again. But, when they got home, the children were tired. They lay down in the grass where they had been playing, and they all decided to take a nap. They dreamt of bakeries and pies and good things to eat.

*The students will say "good-bye" and "thank you" as you narrate them. Have the students walk out the way they came and try to retrace their steps back to the original starting place of the story. The children will lie down and close their eyes as you narrate it.*

And they knew that they would be going back to that bakery again very, very soon. The end.

Everyone stand up and take a big giant bow.

## FOLLOW-UP ACTIVITIES

### What Kinds of Breads and Pies Do You Like?
In this story, the students made some pies, breads, and cookies. There are many different flavors and kinds. Discuss this with your students. Ask them to give you some examples of the different kinds of pies or breads that might be made at a bakery. You may need to help them. Some to include are apple pie, peach pie, cherry pie, pumpkin bread, and banana bread.

Have each child come up to the performing space. Ask each child to tell you his or her favorite kind of pie or bread. Once the child has given his or her answer, pull a piece of this pretend baked good from behind you and give it to the student to gobble up before heading back to the watching space. This activity is simple, and it will encourage your students to think about their own likes and dislikes. It will instill in them the idea that we each have our own opinions.

## The Baker's Assembly Line.

In this story, all the students worked together to bake things. Is this how they do it in a real bakery? Talk about this with your students. Ask them how they think things really get made in a bakery. Do people really jump on the dough? Do the bakers really jump into the bowl to stir things around? Tell your students that one of the most important things that happens in a bakery is that all the bakers work together to make the baked goods. This is called cooperation. Even if you have introduced this concept to your students before, remind them that cooperation means doing things together.

It's time to make a Baker's Assembly Line. Explain to your students that they are going to use cooperation to make things the way that real bakers do — by each having their own job in a line. Then split your students into groups, and give each group one of the following jobs in the baker's assembly line: mixer, roller, cutter, or oven hand. Each group of students will have their own space to work in. Explain to each group what their job is and who they will bring the finished products to before starting over. For example, when the rollers have rolled out some dough, they should run over to the cutters to have the dough cut into cookie shapes before the cutters run over to the oven hands to have the cookies put into the oven. Then begin the assembly line. You may need to cheer them on and get them moving. What you should see after a moment will be children working and running back and forth to their stations. It will look like a bit of chaos. But the more activity going on in the space, the more fun the students will be having. In addition, they will be learning that by doing their own small part in this activity, they are helping to make something together by cooperating.

## Cookie Shapes.

As the students learned, cookies come in all different shapes and sizes. Ask your students if any of them have ever baked real cookies. If so, what shapes did they make? Were they round? Were they heart-shaped? What other shapes have they seen cookies come in?

Sit in a circle with your students. Explain to them that you have an imaginary piece of cookie dough in your hands. Flatten it out on the floor and tell them what shape you are going to make your cookie. Then cut it out of your imaginary dough, peel it up, and gobble it. Then pass the dough around the circle, giving each student a chance to do the same. Each child should take his or her turn, flattening out the dough, telling the class what shape he or she will make, and cutting it out. The reward is eating it at the end. This activity will encourage your students' sense of creativity and individuality, while providing fun for them.

# Discovery Day

## OBJECTIVES

- To introduce the concept of discovery to the students
- To expand the students' imaginations

## STORY SYNOPSIS

A group of children learned that it was Discovery Day — a time to find new things. So, they got into a helicopter and flew to a place called Mexico to see what they could discover. While looking through their binoculars, they saw some people called archeologists who were digging in the ground. The kids decided to help them. They learned that the archeologists were looking for dinosaur bones. The children spent all day digging and searching, but they could not find any dinosaur bones. Finally, after sitting down to eat their lunches and searching some more, they found a real dinosaur bone. They carefully brushed the dirt off and put it in a safe spot so it wouldn't get harmed. Now that they had discovered something, they could go home. A few days later, the children received invitations in the mail inviting them to come to the museum where their dinosaur bone would be displayed. They went and saw their discovery put together with many other dinosaur bones that created a giant T-Rex skeleton. The children felt proud. They couldn't wait until next year's Discovery Day so that they could do it all over again.

## NARRATOR

Once upon a time some kids were running around and playing together, when _____ ran over and said, "Guess what? Today is Discovery Day!" All the children looked very confused and said, "What's a discovery?" So, _____ said, "It's when you find something new!" And the kids all said, "Oh." They huddled together to talk about it and they decided to go somewhere to do some discovering.

> *Have the children come into the performing space and run around for a bit as though they were in the middle of a game. Then insert a student's name into the first blank space in the story. This will prompt that child to repeat the line after you. The other students will repeat the next line after you say it. Make sure that they put on their confused faces as they do. In the second blank space, put the first child's name into the story again. Once all the lines have been said, the students will follow your narration and stand in a circle together for their huddle.*

They packed their backpacks full of things they would need. They put in shovels, binoculars, food, and water. Then all the kids shouted, "Let's go!" and they ran to their helicopter. They got in, put on their helmets and their seat belts, pushed the buttons, and took off. The helicopter made many turns before it finally landed in a hot place called Mexico.

*The children will pack their pretend backpacks as you narrate it. They should all repeat an excited "Let's go!" after you. Then point to where the helicopter is going to be so that your students know where to go. If you've used the car in stories before, it may be helpful to situate the helicopter in the same place for continuity's sake. The children will follow your narration as to how to prepare to fly in the helicopter. Be sure to add some body movement as you turn the aircraft. If you'd like to add another element, you can have the students play with the high temperature of this new place by fanning themselves, putting on sunglasses, or even wiping their brows.*

The children got out and began to look around. They took out their binoculars to see if they could discover anything. Soon they saw some people working, and they decided to go and help them.

*As the children get up, give them a moment to look around and explore. They may soon begin calling out things that they see. Let their imaginations run wild before you bring them back to the story. If you'd like, you can have a student say, "Hey, I see some people," and point in the direction of the archeologists.*

They learned that these people were called archeologists. They are people whose job is to discover things in the ground. One of the archeologists came over and told them that they were looking for old dinosaur bones deep down in the ground. She told them that in some very special places around the world, archeologists have found dinosaur bones.

*You can have the archeologist be an imaginary character, or you can decide to play the role yourself. If you play the part, there's no need to narrate this section in the third person. You can say this section of the story as though the archeologist were informing the children of these facts.*

So the children decided to help. They took out their shovels and started to dig. They worked all day. Sometimes the children thought that they'd found some dinosaur bones. But, when they looked more closely, they realized the bones were from ordinary animals and not dinosaurs at all.

*The moment the students begin to dig, their excitement will take over and they will call out that they've found something. Simply continue by narrating about how the children were fooled by finding other animal bones.*

Finally, it was time for lunch. They took out their lunches from their bags and ate them quietly. The children were getting sad. They thought that they definitely would've found some dinosaur bones by now. This discovering thing was much harder than they thought.

*Let your students find their own space in the room that will be their lunch spots. They will quiet down when they hear this part of your narration. Make sure that they put on their sad faces to show their disappointment.*

When they were done with their lunches, they started digging again in different places. All of a sudden, the children stopped! They looked closely at what they had found, and they all yelled, "We found one!"

*If you would like some additional activities, you can have the students get involved in really cleaning up after themselves at their lunch spots by having them find a pretend trash can and looking for litter on the ground. Then, as you narrate, the students will begin digging again. They will freeze when they hear the section about stopping. They should all repeat the line after you very loudly and excitedly.*

All the archeologists ran over to look. They gave the students special brushes to brush off the dirt from the bones. Sure enough, the children had found a dinosaur leg, and they all jumped up and down and said, "Hooray!" The children carefully took the dinosaur leg and put it in a safe spot so it wouldn't break.

*If you acted as the archeologist, give out the brushes to the students. Have them gently brush off the dinosaur leg. Look for their excited faces as they jump and cheer. It's a great time for cooperation as the students all carefully carry the dinosaur leg to a place that you point to.*

Now that they had discovered something, it was time to go home. The children said good-bye to their archeologist friends and got back into their helicopter. They put on their helmets and their seat belts, pressed all the buttons, and took off. After making some turns, they landed back at home. They were so tired that as soon as they went to their rooms, they lay down and went to sleep.

*Have the students say good-bye. Then they should return to the same spot that the helicopter was in at the beginning of the story and follow your directions for takeoff and flight. Once they land, have them walk toward the center of the space to lie down and sleep.*

A few days later, all the kids opened their mailboxes and found invitations from the archeologists. The dinosaur bones that they had helped to discover were going to be put in a museum. The children were all invited to go see them. So they put on their nice clothes and went to the museum. When they walked in, they were amazed. They saw all the dinosaur bones put together to make an enormous T-Rex skeleton. The kids saw the leg bone that they had found, and they felt very good about helping to discover it.

*The children can simply sit up and pretend to open their mailboxes. They will pretend to get dressed as you narrate it. Don't be surprised if all your students want to tell you what they are wearing. You can take this moment to let their individual tastes shine through as you let them describe their outfits. Simply walk a few steps to get to the museum and lead the children in looking up in awe. You can show them where the dinosaur is and let them walk around it as they look for a few moments. It's a calming way to end your story.*

They spent a long time looking at that dinosaur skeleton, and when it was time to go home, they knew that they couldn't wait until next year's Discovery Day so that they could do it all over again. The end.

Everyone stand up and take a big giant bow.

## FOLLOW-UP ACTIVITIES

Your Own Discoveries. In this story, the students learned that to discover something means to find something new. Discuss this with your students. No doubt, they have come to understand this concept just by being a part of this story. But it will help to reinforce the idea by talking about it once more. Have the students repeat the word after you a few times.

Then talk to your students about other things besides dinosaur bones that have been discovered. You may want to start them out with some examples of your own such as new lands, new animals, and so on. Then ask them to think of some of their own examples. Almost any answer will do here, as most everything was new at one time.

Call each child to the performing space. Give that student a moment to walk through the space and explore it for the purpose of making a discovery. Once he or she has finished, ask that student to tell the class what he or she discovered, and let the child show it to everyone. Make sure that everyone gets a chance to do this. Many of the "discoveries" will be things that already exist in our world. You can encourage the students to tell you something that's different about the object that they've found this time. This is a great activity to encourage a bit of individuality, not to mention creativity.

Museum Trip. Many discoveries get put into museums, just like the dinosaur bones in the story. Let's put the students' new things in a museum too! Announce to your students that all their discoveries from the previous activity are going to be put in the Drama Discovery Museum. The class will be taking a trip there. You can show them where the door to the museum is and let them all in.

One by one, you will visit each child's discovery in various places throughout the room. This is a great chance to let the students verbalize a bit more about their amazing discovery. Tour the room as a class. As you come to each child's find, give that student a moment to answer some questions or tell the class some more about the object. Some questions to pose include: Where did you find this? How old is it? What color is it? Does it have a name?

Once the class has visited each child's exhibit, you can say good-bye to the museum and assure the students that they can come and visit whenever they please.

# Trip to the Library

## OBJECTIVES

- To teach students how libraries work
- To explore the fun that books can offer
- To encourage a love of and interest in books

## STORY SYNOPSIS

Some kids took a trip to the library. When they got there, they learned that they needed to be quiet before going into a library. Once they quieted down, the kids all went in. They each ran to get some books and then sat down together. But then an amazing thing started to happen: The kids started literally getting sucked into the stories in the books. First, they got sucked into a book where they became princes and princesses who danced at a ball and ate at a big feast. Next, they got sucked into a book where they became horses that were being chased by some hunters. They hid in the forest and waited for the hunters to pass. Then the children got sucked into a story where they became bears that were being chased by a group of bees. They had to jump into a river to get rid of them. When this story was finished, the children returned to the library. They were getting tired, so they each checked out a book, and they all went home. When they got there, they ran inside to open their books. Just before opening them, all the children took a deep breath to get ready for the next adventure that they would take.

## NARRATOR

Once upon a time some kids were sitting down at school looking at some books. They had looked at these books many times and were beginning to get bored. So _____ said, "I have an idea. Let's go to the library!" All the other children thought that this was a great idea, and they all yelled, "Yeah!"

> *Have all the students come into the performing space and sit down as though they are reading some books. As you narrate, make sure that they put on their bored faces. Then insert one student's name into the blank space in the story. This will prompt that student to repeat the line after you. The rest of the students should repeat "yeah!" following your narration.*

The children quickly ran outside to their car and got in. They put on their seat belts, turned the key, pressed all the buttons, and drove away. They turned many corners until finally they were there.

*Point to where the car is going to be so that your students know where to run. If you have used a car in a story before, try to put it in the same place for continuity's sake. The students will follow your directions for preparing for the ride and starting the car. As you turn the corners, make sure to put your body into it. Your students will enjoy the excitement of a twisting car ride.*

The car stopped and the kids slowly got out of the car. Just before they opened the door to the library, _____ whispered, "Remember, we have to be quiet in a library".

*The children will slowly stand up as you speak. Insert a student's name into the blank space. This will prompt that student to whisper the line after you.*

The children went inside. They ran for the bookshelves to find some new books to look at. As soon as they found them, they sat down at the tables and began to look at these new books. Pretty soon, an amazing thing started to happen: The children began to get sucked into the stories.

*Let the students run throughout the room to find their books. Most likely, they will begin calling out things like "I've got one." Getting the books will excite them. As you narrate, they will sit down with their books and pretend to read. It's fun if you make a sucking noise each time the children are sucked into a story.*

First, they got sucked into a story where they became princes and princesses. They looked around and saw a big, beautiful castle. They danced with each other at a ball and ate big plates of delicious food. When the story ended, they looked around and found themselves in the library again.

*Give your students a moment to take on the roles of princes and princesses. Let them explore how these characters walk and talk to each other. Then, as you narrate, they will dance around the room. If you have access to music in the space you are working in, now is a great time to make use of it. Turn it on and let them dance for a minute or two. Once they've been to their ball, allow them to sit down at their feast. If you like, take a moment to ask each student what he or she is eating at this royal feast. When the story ends, the students can stand up and become themselves again.*

The children opened another book. This time when they got sucked into the story, they became a herd of horses and ponies. The animals galloped around together, but soon hunters were chasing them. The horses and ponies ran into the woods and hid. They were very quiet, and the hunters passed by them. They all sighed in relief and galloped back to their stables. All of a sudden, the story was over, and the children found themselves in the library again.

*Let the horses and ponies gallop around the room for a moment to allow the students to establish what they have become. As you narrate the chase, the students will delight in running around the room. Point to a corner for them to hide in and make sure that they stay very quiet while the imaginary hunters pass them by. Again, when the story is over, they can stand up and become themselves once more.*

So they opened another book, and soon they were sucked into a new story. This time they were mommy and daddy bears having a picnic. They sat down together and ate their honey. But, before long, a group of bees came by to eat the honey. The bears stood up and tried to swat the bees away, but the bees swarmed around them. The bears had nothing to do but run to the river and jump in. They jumped in with a big splash, and the bees flew away. The bears were so happy that they sat in the water for a while and splashed one another for fun. When this story ended, the children were back in the library one more time.

*Let the bears have a moment to do their usual roaring, and then have them sit down for their picnic. They may want to tell you about some other things they are eating. The bears should stand up and swat away the bees as you narrate it. They will then run toward the river and make a big leap as they jump in. Give them a few moments to splash around in the water before ending this section. When the story ends, the students will stand up and become themselves for the last time.*

They were very tired from their adventures, so they decided not to open any more books for the time being. Instead, they would get some different books to borrow from the library and take home. So, the children walked around the library and chose one book each. Once they had chosen their books, the kids went to the librarian and gave her their library cards. She checked the books out for them and told them to bring the books back next week. They all quietly waved good-bye to her and walked out the door into their car.

*Once more, let the students run around the room to look for their favorite books. The librarian can be an imaginary player in this story, or you may choose to be her. If you play the part, make sure that the students come to you once they have chosen their books. As the librarian, you can take their library cards and stamp their books. When all the books have been checked out, continue your narration, and the students will say "good-bye" as they walk back to the car.*

The children put on their seat belts, turned the key, pressed the buttons, and drove back to school. When they got back to the school, they ran inside to open their books. Just before opening them, all the children took a deep breath to get ready for the next adventure they would take.

*Your students will follow the same directions as before as to how the car starts. Direct the children to return to the watching space. Then, just before opening their books, the students will follow your narration and take a deep breath.*

The end. Everyone stand up and take a big giant bow.

# FOLLOW-UP ACTIVITIES

**What's Your Favorite Book?** In this story, the students got to read and look at many different books from a library. Do any of the students have a favorite book? Talk to your students about some of the books that they have read either with their parents at home or during story time at school. Ask them to give you examples of some of these books. Call each child to the performing space. Ask that student to tell the class about his or her favorite book. This activity will allow your students to stand up in front of their peers while encouraging an interest in reading and books.

**Buying and Borrowing.** In the story, the children went to a library. What is the difference between a library and a bookstore? Pose this question to your students and discuss. Let them brainstorm the answer together before letting them know that at a bookstore people buy books and at a library they borrow them. Remind them that when a person borrows a book, he or she also has to bring it back.

Ask your students to show you the books they borrowed in the story. You may want to go around the room and ask each student what book he or she took out. Once you've done this, let your students know that a week has passed and it's time to return their library books. Take a walk or a car ride (or any other mode of transportation you wish) to the library. If you played the librarian in the story, take on this role again as the students form a line to return their books. Make sure that you stamp each child's book and thank the class for coming to the library again. You can stop the activity here, or you can allow your students to take out another book to show them what an endless resource a library can be. Then return to school once more and congratulate them on being such good library members.

**Pictures Tell Stories Too.** When a student reads a book with his or her parents or teachers, are the students just listening to the words or are there pictures too? Discuss this with your students. Undoubtedly at this age, all the books that they are reading have pictures in them, and these pictures also help to tell the story. Give them some examples using some of your learning center's most popular books.

Then sit in a circle with the class. Invite them to lie on their stomachs and tell them they are about to draw some imaginary pictures. Hand out sheets of imaginary paper and tell them that they are going to draw pictures that help to tell the story of the trip they just took. Let the students know that they are free to draw a picture of any one thing from the story that they wish. Give them about thirty seconds to come up with an idea and flesh it out. Once they've finished, go around the circle and ask each student to tell the class which part of the story he or she drew. Have them show their drawings to the class, and make sure that each child gets a turn. If you wish to end the activity here, you've already encouraged your students to use their imaginations to make stories come to life.

You can continue the activity by collecting your students' imaginary pictures and retelling an abridged version of the story. Use the children's drawings to tell the story, and hold up each one as it becomes appropriate. It may seem silly to have your students staring at a bunch of imaginary pictures, but they will believe every second of it. In addition, this activity will empower them and give them the feeling that they can make stories, too.

# As We Crawl Through a Cave

## OBJECTIVES

- To teach students about natural caves
- To encourage kindness to others

## ROLES FOR STUDENTS TO CHOOSE FROM

| Role | Selling Point for the Students |
| --- | --- |
| Raccoons | Gets to act smart and cute |
| Bats | Gets to fly around |
| Spiders | Gets to crawl around and spin webs |
| Bears | Gets to act big and fierce but also kind and sleepy |

This adventure story is unique in that your students can play other roles besides children. However, you will need some of your students to act as kids in this story, so if you need to sell this idea to them, make it enticing by letting them choose a new name or some traits that they would like to have.

## STORY SYNOPSIS

Some kids found a cave and decided to go inside and explore. First, they met some Raccoons that slept in the cave during the day and came out to play with their friends at night. They told the kids that the animals in the cave wouldn't bother them if the kids didn't bother the animals. Next the kids met a Bear that was sleeping there with his family. As the children walked deeper into the cave, they also met Bats that sleep upside down and a Spider that was weaving a web. After exploring the whole cave, the children found their way out again. They rubbed their eyes from the bright sunlight and wandered back to their own homes. Animals may live in caves, but these kids still liked living in houses.

## NARRATOR

Once upon a time some kids were playing outside in the woods. They saw a mountain nearby, and they decided to climb it. They began to climb, and climb, and climb even higher. All of sudden, the children all yelled, "Look! A cave!"

*Call all the students who are playing children into the performing space. As you narrate, they will begin their pretend climb. You may have to show them how to mime this if you notice that they are not getting the hang of it. Give them a spot to point to as they as they repeat the line after you.*

Some of the children were excited, but others were scared. All of them thought that it might be neat to see what animals lived inside the cave.

*Encourage your students to say why they think the cave might be scary and why it might be fun.*

Finally the children had made up their minds. They were going in. They all put on their hard hats with flashlights on top and shouted, "Let's go!" They slowly walked toward the entrance. When they crawled inside the cave, the children could feel the air get colder. They looked around and wondered who could possibly live there

*The children will put on their hard hats as you narrate it. Then they will excitedly repeat the line after you. Show them where the entrance to the cave is so that they all walk there together. Then make sure that they get down on their knees to crawl inside. Once they are inside, give them a moment to play with the idea of the cold air.*

All of a sudden, they saw some Raccoons. At first the children were scared and ran over to a corner to hide. But the Raccoons walked over to them and said, "Don't be afraid. We won't hurt you as long as you don't hurt us." This made the children feel better. The Raccoons explained, "We sleep in the cave during the day. Then at night, we go out and look for food and see our raccoon friends." The children then realized they were standing on the Raccoons' bed. They said, "Sorry," and moved on through the cave.

*Call your Raccoons to the performing space. As you narrate it, the children will scatter throughout the room and hide. Make sure that they put on their scared faces. Then break up the Raccoons' lines into small sections so that the children playing these roles will be able to repeat the lines after you. Once the children step off the beds and apologize, the Raccoons can return to their seats.*

As they walked further in, they saw a giant Bear. This time the children were very scared. A bear could really hurt them. When the Bear saw the kids, he said, "Don't be scared. I'm just sleeping. If you don't hurt me, I won't hurt you." The children all agreed that they didn't want to hurt the Bear, and the Bear lay back down and continued sleeping.

*Call your Bears to the performing space. If possible, don't let them indulge in the usual bear roars. We want these to be nice friendly Bears. Your students can run to a different part of the room to hide from the Bears. Then have the Bears repeat their lines after you. After this exchange with the children, the Bears can lie down and go to sleep. Direct the Bears back to their seats.*

Then the students walked even further into the cave. It was starting to get dark. So the kids turned on the flashlights attached to their hats. They looked around, and when they looked up, they saw Bats hanging upside down. The Bats were sleeping. One of them woke up when the children flashed their flashlights on him. He flew down to talk to them. He told the kids, "We sleep up here during the day because we don't like daylight. At night, we come out and look for food." The kids promised not to disturb the Bats, and the Bat flew back up to the ceiling, hung upside down, and went back to sleep.

*As you narrate, the children will walk on. Make sure that they reach up and turn on their hard hat lights. Call the Bats to the performing space. Let them fly around for a moment (as this is part of the fun of being a bat) before finding their upside-down sleeping position. An easy way to create this illusion for your students is to have them lie down with their feet up against the wall. Then, upon your narration, one or all of them can fly down toward the children. Have the Bats repeat their lines after you and then fly back to their resting spots. Once their section is finished, they can return to their seats.*

As they walked further in, the children saw what they had been dreading: Spiders. Many of the kids were scared. But, as they looked closer, they saw that the Spiders were not there to hurt them. They were busy spinning their webs. They spun beautiful webs of silk and sat inside them, waiting to catch some food. The children decided that they should not bother these Spiders. They remembered what the Raccoons and the Bears had said: "If you don't bother us, we won't bother you." So they decided to leave the Spiders alone.

*Give the children a chance to explore deeper into the cave. Then call your Spiders to the space. When the children see the Spiders, they should back away a bit and put on their scared faces. Your Spiders can then begin crawling in circles as they weave their webs. You may need to do this with them so that they get the idea. When their section is finished, the Spiders can return to their seats.*

It was getting late, and it was time for the children to crawl out of the cave. They passed the Bats, the Bears, and the Raccoons again. Finally the children reached the entrance to the cave. When they crawled out, they rubbed their eyes for a moment. The sun seemed very bright to them after being in such a dark cave. They turned off their flashlights, took off their hard hats, and headed back down the mountain. When they got back to their homes, the children opened the doors to their houses and stepped inside. They closed their eyes, went to sleep, and dreamt of the next cave that they would get to explore.

*Have the children crawl back the way that they came. As they pass the other animals, you may wish to have them say good-bye to each set. Then as you narrate their exit, they should stand up and rub their eyes. They will follow your instructions as they take off their gear and head down the mountain. Then let them open their doors, lie down, and pretend to sleep in the middle of the space.*

Animals may live in caves, but these kids still liked living in houses. The end.

Everyone stand up and take a big giant bow.

# FOLLOW-UP ACTIVITIES

## Being Kind to Others.

In this story, the raccoons and the bears taught the children a very important lesson: by acting nicely to others, others will act nicely in return. Discuss this with your students in terms of kindness to animals. For example, you may want to talk about stepping on ants, pulling the legs off spiders, or chasing and yelling at birds (a favorite pastime among some children of this age). Then move your discussion on toward kindness to other people. Talk with your students about why it's good to be nice to others.

Call each student up to the performing space. Ask that child what he or she can do to be kind to a friend. The answers may be as simple as sharing a toy or the answers may get more complex. The point is for your students to think up their own acts of kindness and to share these in front of their peers.

## The Different Parts of a Cave.

In the story, the animals lived in different parts of the cave. Why might they do this? Pose this question to your students. Let them brainstorm as a class as they try to figure out why these animals live in different parts of the cave. Encourage them to think about how dark it got as they crawled further in. Let your students know about the sections of a cave. The one closest to the entrance is for animals that are just looking for shelter but still go outside to get their food. But the animals that live farther back in the cave, where there is no light, don't leave the cave for food. They live inside the cave all the time, and some of them can't see at all.

Ask your students to choose which way they think would be the most fun and interesting way to live: going in and out of the cave, or living one's whole life inside a cave. Then, once they have decided, split them into the two groups of inhabitants, letting them decide which kind of animal to be.

It's time to make a pretend cave. Call all the students to the performing space. Show them where the entrance to the cave is and where the back of the cave is. Tell your students that their main goals are to get food and to make friends. Then it's time to let the animals live their lives. The ones who live at the front of the cave can leave the cave to get their food and can come back inside when they want to sleep and see their friends. The ones at the back of the cave must look around inside the cave for plants and tiny insects that they can eat. These animals cannot go too close to the front of the cave because the light will hurt their eyes. The parameters of this activity are wide open. Let your students play this out for a few minutes. The most important thing is for them to interact with one another while learning just how the life of a cave truly works.

After the activity, you may want to take a moment to go around the room and ask each child what it felt like to live in his or her part of the cave. Was it exciting? Was it lonely? Did he or she make lots of friends? This will give the children a little closure and one more opportunity to voice opinions and thoughts of their own.

# Trip to the Clothing Store

## OBJECTIVES

- To promote decision-making skills
- To encourage creativity and individuality

## STORY SYNOPSIS

Some children went clothes shopping with their mommies. They tried on pants and shirts. They ran through the store picking out different things that they liked, and they tried them on in the fitting rooms. When they'd made their decisions, the children brought their new clothes to the cash register and paid for them. Then they went home and put them away. A few days later, the children were invited to a party. So they opened their closets and drawers and chose something nice to wear. They went to the party, danced, and ate cake. The children were happy that they got to choose what to wear that day, and they had a very good time with their friends. When they lay down to go to sleep, they hoped that they could do it all over again very soon.

## NARRATOR

Once upon a time some kids were playing in their rooms. Their mommies came in to tell them that it was time to go shopping at the clothing store. The children thought that this was a great idea, and they all yelled, "Hooray!" They put on their jackets, closed the door, and ran to the car.

> *Call all your students to the performing space and let them play with each other for a moment to let them get established in the world of the story. You can make the role of the mother an imaginary player, or you can choose to play the role yourself. It's best not to have a student play this role in this particular story because they will miss out on the action and the learning. Your students will loudly shout "hooray!" after you. Point to where the car will be so that your students know where to go. If you've used a car in earlier stories, try to put it in the same location for continuity's sake.*

They got in, put on their seat belts, turned the key, pressed all the buttons, and drove off toward the clothing store. They had to make some turns and some stops, but pretty soon they were there. The kids took off their seat belts and got out of the car. They looked both ways, crossed the street, and walked into the store.

*Your students will follow your directions as to what to do in the car (although, if you've used this action before, they will undoubtedly know the drill as well as you do). Put your body into the turns and stops and have your students do the same. It will make the car ride exciting. You can all look both ways together and then cross the street as you walk into the store.*

Inside, they stopped and looked around for a moment. There was so much clothing! They exclaimed, "How will we ever choose?" So they started to look around. The kids looked at all the different clothes.

*It's nice to slow this section down a bit to give it a sense of wonder and awe. You really want to have your students believe that the store is huge. Your students will repeat the line after you. Then encourage them to look throughout the performing space as they scope out the store.*

They tried on some pants and looked in the mirror to see if the pants fit. Then they tried on some shirts and looked in the mirror. Then they ran through the store picking out lots and lots of clothing. Once they had piles of clothes in their arms, they started trying them all on.

*As you narrate, the children will try on the pants and the shirts. Again, let them use the whole space as they run through the store picking out piles of clothing. Make sure that their arms are weighed down with all the imaginary things that they are carrying. They should carry them back to their original fitting-room spots and begin trying all the clothes on. Give them a moment or two to do this, as this is dress-up time in their minds.*

After a long while, the children had made their decisions. They took their clothes up to the register and waited in line. At the checkout register, the clerk told each of them how much they owed. One by one, the children reached into their pockets for their money and paid for their new clothes. Once they were finished, they waited in the car.

*It's helpful for you to play the clerk at the checkout counter. Your students will make a line to pay you. Take your time and deal with each student individually. Tell them how much it will be and let them dig into their pockets to pay you. They're dying to feel grown up enough to pay for things. So let them each have their moment. After each child has paid, he or she can wait in the car for the rest of the students.*

At last, after a long day of shopping, it was time to go home. The children put on their seat belts, turned the key, pressed all the buttons, and drove away from the store with their mommies. When they got home, they ran into the house and up to their rooms. There they put away all their new clothes in their closets and drawers. Then they lay down and took a nap. It's exhausting to be out all day trying things on.

*Once all the children are in the car again, they will follow your instructions about starting it. Let them run into their imaginary houses and put away all their clothing. You may want to encourage them to be gentle with and take good care of their new clothing. Then let them lie down right where they are for their nap.*

A few days later, the children went to a party. They woke up and went right to their closets to pick out what to wear. Now was their chance to wear some of the new clothing. They put on their clothes and brushed their hair. Once they were finished, they left for the party.

*Let the children wake up and go straight for the closets. They will pick out what to wear and put it on. Again, this is like a giant game of dress-up for them, so indulge them for a moment or two as they get themselves ready.*

When they got to the party, all their friends were there. The children danced and played for a very long time. They sat down and ate some cake with their friends. When it was time to go home, they all said good-bye and went back to their homes.

*Let the students greet one another. They may start telling each other what they are wearing. If not, you don't need to force it. There will be plenty of time in the follow-up activities to find out what choices they've made. If you have access to music in your space, now is a great time to use it. Turn it on and let the students dance for a few moments at the party. As you narrate, the children will sit down and gobble up some cake. Then let them say good-bye to all their friends before leaving the party.*

At home, the children took off their clothes, put on their pajamas, and got into bed. The children were very happy that they got to choose what to wear that day and had such a good time with their friends.

*Let your students take their pretend clothes off and put on their imaginary pajamas. Once they've done this, they can lie down on the floor and listen to the remainder of the story.*

As they lay down to go to sleep, they hoped that they could do it all over again very soon. The end.

Everyone stand up and take a big giant bow.

## FOLLOW-UP ACTIVITIES

### What Did You Buy?
In this story, the students went to a clothing store and picked out their own clothes. What did they buy? Sit in a circle with your students. Go around the circle and ask each child to describe one thing that he or she bought on the imaginary trip to the clothing store. Let them be as descriptive as they like.

Then go around once more. This time, ask each student to tell the class what he or she picked out of his or her imaginary closets to wear to the party. This is a great chance to let your students make decisions while indulging the world of their imaginations.

**Money, Money, Money.** In this story, the students used their own pretend money to buy the clothes they wanted. Do they always use money to buy things? Discuss this with your students. Most likely, they have gone to the store with their parents enough times to know that people need money to buy things. Some of your students may offer up how much they've got saved in a piggy bank, and that's great. It means that they are learning to respect money. What your students probably don't understand is that there is not always an endless supply. The next activity will help them to grasp that concept.

Tell your students that they have a little bit of money left from their shopping spree. Now they are in a new store, and they only have enough to buy one of the following items: a stuffed animal, a game, or some candy. Then call each child to the performing space. Ask that student which of these three things he or she will choose to buy. Once they've made their decision, make an imaginary exchange of the item for money, and let them return to their seat. This activity not only teaches the students about the limits of money, but it also encourages your students to continue to make their own decisions.

**Let's Make Some Clothes.** Usually, people buy their clothes. If the students could make their own clothes, what would the clothes look like? Discuss this with your students. You may want to include the concept of designers and clothing-makers in your discussion. Explain to your students how someone first draws a picture of what the clothes will look like and then they make them.

It's time for each student to make his or her own shirt. Have your students spread out throughout the space. Explain to them that you are giving each of them a piece of imaginary fabric and paints. They will cut out their own shirts and design them however they please. Give them a few moments to really make their creations complete. Once they've finished, go around the room and ask each child to describe his or her new shirt to the rest of the class. Once everyone has had a chance, let all the students put on their new shirts and look in the pretend mirror. It will empower your students to create something like this on their own.

# Day at an Aquarium

## OBJECTIVES

- To teach students the functions of aquariums
- To explore the worlds of underwater animals
- To encourage creativity and individuality

## STORY SYNOPSIS

Some children went to an aquarium. There they swam with dolphins, took a very slow ride on the backs of some sea turtles, carefully fed the sharks, and helped keep the baby penguins warm while the mommy and daddy penguins were being fed. At the end of the day, they went back to school and looked at their fish tank. This time they understood a little bit more about the animals that live underwater. And, as they looked at their underwater friends, they hoped that they would be able to visit another aquarium very, very soon.

## NARRATOR

Once upon a time some kids were standing around their fish tank at school looking at the fish. All of a sudden, _____ said, "I have an idea. Let's go to an aquarium." The rest of the kids put on their confused faces and asked, "What's an aquarium?" And _____ explained, "It's like a zoo for fish." Well the kids thought that this was a great idea, and they all cheered, "Let's go!"

*Call all the students to the performing space to look at the imaginary fish tank. Let them observe for a moment. They may begin to call out things that they see in it, and that is great. It means that they are giving their imaginations over to the world of the story. Insert one student's name into the blank space in the story. This will prompt that child to repeat the line after you. Then the rest of your students will repeat the question. Have the same child as before say the answer. Then all the students will cheer "Let's go!"*

They ran out to their car and hopped in. They put on their seat belts, turned the key, pressed all the buttons, and drove off. The children had to make some turns to get there, but finally they stopped the car and got out. They walked into the aquarium and bought their tickets. Now they could go see the animals.

*Point to where the car is going to be so that your students all know where to go. If you have used the car before in your stories, they will likely know exactly where to go. They will follow your instructions about starting the car. Make sure to put your body into the movements of the trav-*

*eling car so that your students will follow your example. You may choose to have the students buy the admission tickets from you or from an imaginary person.*

First, they walked over to see the dolphins. The dolphins were swimming around in an enormous pool, and the kids watched them for a moment. Then one of the aquarium workers walked over to the children and asked them the best question that they had ever heard. He asked, "Hey kids, would you like to swim with the dolphins?" The children could hardly contain their excitement. They jumped up and down and said, "We would, we would!"

*Point to where the dolphin tank will be so that your students know where to walk. Then give them a moment to watch the dolphins swimming. It's best if you play the aquarium worker. However, if you do not wish to do this, simply narrate the story with him as an imaginary character. Make sure that your students jump up and down and repeat the line after you.*

So he brought the kids some wet suits. He told them that they had to wear the wet suits to keep themselves warm because dolphins live in cold water. So the children put on the wet suits and zipped them up. They jumped into the dolphin pool and began to swim with the dolphins.

*You may have to put on a wet suit, too, to show your students how it works. Once they have them on, let them jump into the dolphin pool.*

At first the children were a little frightened because the dolphins were much bigger than they thought they would be. But the dolphins swam over to the children and nodded their heads to show that they were nice. The children petted the dolphins. Next they held on to the dolphins' fins, and the dolphins took the children for a swim around the pool. The dolphins swam faster and faster, and they jumped out of the water as the children flew with them into the air.

*Make sure the children put on their scared faces at first. Then, as you narrate the kindness of the dolphins, your students can pet them. They will happily hold onto these pretend dolphins and swim around the room with them. Let them jump out of the water and swim back under again. You may wish to let them do this a couple of times, just because it's so much fun for them.*

Soon the ride was over. The children petted the dolphins one more time and climbed out of the pool. They all yelled, "That was fun!" Then they took off their wet suits, dried off, and put their clothes back on. There was so much more to see.

*The students will pet the dolphins one more time. Then, when they get out, make sure that they repeat the line after you. They will follow your instructions as they take off their wet suits and dry off.*

Next, the children went to see the sea turtles. The turtles lived in a different pool. Some of them were swimming, and some of them were resting on land. The aquarium worker asked the kids if they would like to take a turtle ride. So the children gently climbed onto the turtle shells and went for a ride. But it was not as exciting as they thought it would be. Turtles moved very, very slowly. So, after a few moments, they petted the turtles and climbed off.

*Walk the students to a new part of the room where the sea turtles will be. Because the turtles will not move very much, the children can pretend to climb onto them and actually sit on the floor. This will help to show them how slow a turtle really moves.*

Next they went to the shark tank. It was feeding time for the sharks, and the aquarium worker asked the children if they would like to help feed them. The children were a little scared about this because they knew that sharks have very sharp teeth. But the aquarium worker showed them how to do it carefully. As the sharks came around, the children reached into a bucket of fish and quickly threw the fish toward the sharks. The hungry sharks opened their big mouths and grabbed the food right away. They kept throwing the food in until they had reached the bottom of the bucket. Then they washed their hands and said good-bye to the sharks.

*Walk the students to yet another space to see the sharks. The students should put on their scared faces at first. Then give them each a bucket of fish. As you narrate, they will throw the fish in quickly. It may become a kind of game to them, which is fine; doing this will make it more fun. Once they are finished, they will say good-bye. Then let them wash their hands in an imaginary sink before moving on.*

Next, it was time to visit the penguins. When they got to the penguin tank, they were greeted with a big surprise. Some of the penguins had just had babies. All the penguins were standing around the babies, keeping them warm. But now it was feeding time for the mommy and daddy penguins. So the aquarium worker gave the children a job. While the mommy and daddy penguins were eating, the children huddled around the babies and kept the chicks warm until the parents returned. It was very cold in the penguin room, and the children started shivering. They could see why the parents had to keep the babies warm.

*Walk the students to one more space in the room to see the penguins. As you narrate, the students will stand close together in a huddle to keep the babies warm. They should start shivering as you narrate it.*

Once the mommy and daddy penguins returned, the children were able to leave. When they got outside the tank, the aquarium worker was waiting with some hot chocolate to warm them up and to thank them for their help. The children had had a long day visiting the aquarium, but now it was time to go home.

*The children can quickly run out of the penguin tank to get out of the cold. Then hand them each their own cup of cocoa and let them sip it while they get warm.*

They said good-bye to all their new friends and got back into their car. They put on their seat belts, turned the key, pressed all the buttons, and drove away. They made a couple of big turns, and soon they were back at school. They carefully got out of the car and walked back to their classroom to look at their fish tank again.

*As you narrate, the children will say good-bye to the worker and all the animals. As they sit down in the car, the children will follow your instructions to start it. Once you've stopped the car, they should get out and walk back to where the fish tank was at the beginning of the story.*

This time they understood a little bit more about the animals that live underwater. And, as they looked at their underwater friends, they hoped that they would be able to visit another aquarium very, very soon. The end.

Everyone stand up and take a big giant bow.

## FOLLOW-UP ACTIVITIES

### Naming the Babies.
In the story, the students got to meet the baby penguins. Do the students think the baby penguins all had names? Discuss this with your students. Tell them that at zoos and aquariums the animals usually do have names. This helps the zookeepers and aquarium workers keep track of the different animals, and it helps the scientists study them. Take a moment to explain to your students that aquariums are not just places for people to come and see the animals. They are also places where scientists work to learn about these different animals and how they live.

Then tell your students that you just got a call from the aquarium and the turtles just had ten new babies (or one for however many children you have in your class), and they all need names. Call each child up to the performing space and ask that student to name one of the turtles. This activity will teach them a bit more about the function of an aquarium while giving them chances to use a little of their own creativity and express their individuality.

### Save a Whale.
The scientists that work at an aquarium are called marine biologists. Some of the animals they bring to an aquarium are animals they had to save in the wild. Discuss this with your students. Ask them why they think some of these animals would need to be saved. You may wish to talk about how some animals get hurt in the water and cannot help themselves.

Tell your students that they are about to spend the day with a marine biologist. They just got a call that a dolphin is hurt in the ocean, and they have to go and save it. Then have all the students come to the performing space and run to the beach where the dolphin has been brought in. Once they are there, have everyone help to load this heavy dolphin into the back of a truck. (You and I know that children would never be able to lift a dolphin, but the students will readily go along with this idea, and it will help to empower them through this activity.) Then, as you ride in the truck back to the aquarium, explain to the students that dolphins need to be kept wet or they will die. Give the students imaginary buckets of water and rags. Have them dip the rags in water and rub the dolphin down with them. Make sure that they work together and check in with them every couple of seconds to make sure the dolphin is OK. After a few moments, they will unload the dolphin from the truck and bring him to a pool at the aquarium. Once he is safe, thank them for their help and let them return to their seats.

You may wish to follow this activity by asking your students how that made them feel. Most of your students will feel pretty good knowing that they just helped save an animal. Remind them that this is what marine biologists have to do sometimes in addition to their jobs at the aquarium.

# UNIT 5
# Moral Lessons

Each story in this unit is designed to teach your students a moral lesson. Some deal with basics such as sharing, listening, and grabbing. Others deal with more specific problems that children of this age often face, like eating habits and transitions.

Role selection in these stories can be done quite strategically. If one of your students is dealing with the particular problem that your story is addressing, consider encouraging that child to play the role that reveals the moral, such as a parent. This helps the student to learn the lesson from a positive viewpoint without feeling punished.

It's helpful to tell the moral stories with your students on a regular basis. The more familiar your students are with the lessons that these stories teach, the easier it is for them to access those themes the rest of the day. You will be amazed as you watch your students remind each other of the lesson that they learned from a moral story from drama.

# The Bear and the Tiger

## OBJECTIVES

- To encourage students to share
- To learn about the alternatives to hitting others

## ROLES FOR STUDENTS TO CHOOSE FROM

| Role | Selling Point for the Students |
|---|---|
| Baby Bear | Gets to act scary |
| Baby Tiger | Gets to act big and strong |
| Mommy or Daddy Bear | Gets to act like a mommy or daddy |
| Mommy or Daddy Tiger | Gets to act like a mommy or daddy |

## STORY SYNOPSIS

In a big, big forest, a giant rock stood high over all the other rocks. One day, a Baby Bear and a Baby Tiger found this rock at the same time. They each climbed to the top, and when they saw each other, they growled. They each wanted the rock for themselves. After growling and roaring, the Baby Bear and the Baby Tiger started to use their claws. But after a few moments, they both got hurt and ran home. The Mommy Bear was very angry that the Baby Bear had used his claws. She told him that it's not OK to fight with claws and that tomorrow he would have to apologize to the Tiger. The Mommy Tiger was also upset. She told the Baby Tiger that next time he would have to share. The next day, the Baby Bear and the Baby Tiger met at the rock again. The Baby Bear apologized, and the Baby Tiger suggested that they share the rock since it was so big. Pretty soon the Baby Bear and the Baby Tiger met on the rock every day and became best friends. And they never used their claws to solve problems ever again.

## NARRATOR

Once upon a time, in a big, big forest, there was a giant rock. It stood high over all the other rocks and was big enough for any animal to climb. One day a Bear was out in the woods playing bear games. The same day, a Tiger was playing in the same woods on the other side of the rock. All of a sudden, the Bear and the Tiger stopped and looked up. There, for the first time, they saw the enormous, gigantic climbing rock. Both of them said, "I want to climb it!" So they began to climb. They climbed and climbed until they reached the top at exactly the same time.

*As you introduce their characters, call the Bear to the space and then the Tiger. Give them a moment to run around and play their animal games. They should stop and look up as you narrate it. However, you may need to do this, too, to get them engaged in the action. The Bear and the Tiger should both repeat the line after you and then begin to climb. When they reach the top, they should be facing one another for the showdown.*

When they saw each other, the Bear roared. They each wanted the rock for themselves. So the Bear said, "This rock is mine." And the Tiger replied, "No, it's mine." They went back and forth arguing about the rock until they started fighting with their paws and their claws. Both of them got hurt, and both the Bear and the Tiger ran all the way home.

*As you narrate, the students will roar and growl. Then have them repeat their lines after you. It's always fun to keep the argument going for a bit longer. This may mean that you have to add extra lines for them to repeat, or your students may already be arguing without your help. The argument can continue quite simply with "Mine" shouted back and forth by both parties. Once the physical fighting begins, make sure to remind your students that this is a pretend fight and that they should not actually be hitting one another. It's helpful to address this point before you even begin telling the story. As they run all the way home, the children can return to their seats.*

When the Bear got back to his cave, his Mommy and Daddy said, "What happened?" So the Bear explained what happened at the rock. The Mommy Bear and Daddy Bear shook their heads and said, "Fighting is not OK. You have to use your words." The Bear tried to argue with them about it, but the Mommy Bear and Daddy Bear wouldn't hear of it. They told him that tomorrow he would have to go back to that rock and apologize to the Tiger. Then they cleaned up his cuts, put some bandages on him, and sent him to bed.

*Have the Bear come back into the space. Call the Mommy and Daddy Bears to the space as well. The parents will say their line once you've narrated it. Make sure that they shake their heads in disappointment. They can even add a little "tsk, tsk, tsk" as well. Then they will repeat their second line. The Bear should try to tell them his side of the story. You may have him say, "But, but, but" to try and sway his parents. The Mommy and Daddy Bears will fix up his cuts, then they can all return to their seats.*

When the Tiger got home, his Mommy and Daddy said, "What happened?" So the Tiger explained all about the fight at the rock. The Mommy Tiger and Daddy Tiger just shook their heads and said, "You can't have it all to yourself. You have to share." The Tiger tried to argue with them about it, but they wouldn't listen. They told the Tiger that tomorrow he would have to go back to the rock and share with the Bear. Then they cleaned up his cuts, put on some bandages, and sent him to bed.

*Call all the Tigers to the performing space. Have the parents repeat their first line after you. Then, as you narrate, they should shake their heads and show their disappointment. They will repeat their second line to the Tiger while he tries to argue in the same way that the Bear did. Then let the parents put on some bandages and everyone can return to their seats.*

The next morning, the Bear and the Tiger went to the rock. They climbed up the sides and got to the top at exactly the same time again. But this time they did not growl and roar. The Bear said, "I'm sorry we fought." And the Tiger said, "Why don't we share the rock. It's big enough." The Bear looked around and noticed that the rock was big enough for both of them. So he said, "OK," and they shook paws on it.

*Call the Bear and the Tiger to the performing space again. Have them stand on opposite sides of the rock and then begin their climb to the top. The Bear will make his apology and the Tiger will offer his solution as they repeat the lines after you. Always remember to break up any lines that are too long so that your students will not have to remember too much at one time. Let the Bear take a moment to look around and realize how big the rock is. Once he agrees, make sure that the two shake hands or give a high-five. Then they can sit down on top of the rock.*

The Bear and the Tiger met each other every day at that rock and quickly became best friends. They even invited their parents to come and have a picnic on the rock with them.

*Have all the mommies and daddies come to the performing space and climb up onto your imaginary rock. You can choose to have an elaborate picnic, or you can simply acknowledge it through your narration.*

For many, many years after that, the Bear and the Tiger were best friends because they shared things. And they never used their paws or their claws to fight with each other ever again. The end.

Everyone stand up and take a big giant bow.

## FOLLOW-UP ACTIVITIES

**To Hit or Not to Hit.** In this story, the Bear and the Tiger do something that is not OK: They use their paws to fight with one another. Is it ever OK to fight with someone? What should children do instead? Discuss this with your students and ask them these questions. Undoubtedly, your school or learning center has addressed these questions with the students many, many times. But you're probably well aware that it can never hurt to refresh their memories.

Then call each student to the performing space. Ask that child whether it's ever all right to hit someone. (Obviously, the answer should be no.) You may wish to give the student an example, such as "If someone takes a toy from you, is it OK to hit him?" Once the child has told you that it's not OK to hit someone, ask him or her what to do instead. When the child has finished, congratulate him or her for remembering the rules and send the child back to his or her seat. Encourage the children to use their words or to talk to a teacher when there is a problem.

### Sharing with Our Friends.
The Bear and Tiger learned how to get along by sharing the rock. What kinds of things do people share? Who do the students share with? Talk about this with your students. Encourage them to give you instances when it's nice to share and with whom they should be sharing things.

Sit in a circle with your students. Explain to them that you have a grab bag full of toys. Go around the circle and let each child pull one out. Then have them tell the class what toy they pulled out and let them show it to everyone. Next, pair your students up to play with each other. Let them know that during this activity, they will have to share with their partner and not fight over toys. They must use their words and they must share. Then let the pairs play with their imaginary toys for a minute or two. Be sure to observe each group, and help the pairs that are having trouble getting along with one another. When time is up, call them back to the circle to discuss their experiences. They will undoubtedly be very proud and excited to let you know the ways in which they shared.

# The Day the Rules Got Forgotten

## OBJECTIVES

- To teach students the importance of obeying rules

## ROLES FOR STUDENTS TO CHOOSE FROM

| Role | Selling Point for the Students |
| --- | --- |
| Little Boy or Little Girl | Gets to horse around and be silly |
| Mommy and/or Daddy | Gets to act like a mommy or daddy |
| Teacher | Gets to tell people what to do |
| A Friend | Gets to play and act smart |
| A Dog | Gets to act like a dog and play games |

This story is written with the Little Girl as the main character. However, if you have a boy who would like to play the part, too, you can either let him play the role as is, or you can add a Little Boy to your narration. The same goes for the roles of the Mommy and Daddy.

## STORY SYNOPSIS

There was a Little Girl who loved to play. She loved to play so much that sometimes she didn't pay attention to the rules. One day she didn't obey when her Mommy told her to eat her breakfast. She played with her dolls instead. And she didn't obey when her Mommy told her to take her lunch box to school with her. She played around with her dog instead. And, on the way to school, the Little Girl didn't stay close to her Mommy at the store like she was supposed to. She went off to look at the candy instead. That day at lunchtime, the Little Girl didn't have a lunch box. She cried and cried because she realized that she hadn't obeyed her Mommy by taking her lunch box to school. The Little Girl's Teacher told her that she would have to pay attention to the rules from now on. For now, the children who had obeyed their parents by bringing their lunch boxes to school shared their lunches with her. And that night, when her Mommy told her it was time for bed, the Little Girl made sure to obey.

# NARRATOR

Once upon a time there was a Little Girl who loved to play. She loved to play so much that sometimes she didn't pay attention to the rules. One day she woke up to go to school. She got dressed and went downstairs where breakfast was waiting for her.

*Call the Little Girl to the performing space and let her run around the room and play for a moment to help establish her character. Then, as you narrate, she should wake up, get dressed, and walk downstairs to breakfast.*

Her Mommy said, "Be sure to eat your breakfast." Then her Mommy went upstairs to finish getting dressed. Well, the Little Girl heard her Mommy but didn't really bother obeying her. The Little Girl was much more interested in taking out her dolls and playing with them. So that's what she did. She spent the rest of the morning playing games and did not eat her breakfast.

*Call the Mommy to the space and have her repeat her line after you. Then she can return to her seat. As you continue your narration, the Little Girl should run over to her dolls and begin to play with them.*

Later, as they were leaving the house, the Little Girl's Mommy said, "Remember to take your lunch." The Little Girl heard her, but she didn't really pay attention to what her Mommy said. She was much more interested in playing with her dog. They played lots of games together, and the Little Girl forgot to take her lunch to school with her.

*Have the Mommy come to the performing space to say her line. She can return to her seat again once she's said it. Then have the dog come into the space to play with the Little Girl. Let them romp around together for a few moments before sending the dog back to his seat.*

On the way to school, the Little Girl and her Mommy held hands and walked down the street on the sidewalk. They stopped inside a store to get some juice, and the Little Girl's Mommy said, "Stay close by and don't wander off." The Little Girl heard this, but she decided not to obey her Mommy. While her Mommy was choosing which juice to get, the Little Girl decided to go look at the candy. She walked through the store, searching and searching. Pretty soon, she looked around and said, "Oh no!" She realized that she was lost, and she wondered how she would ever get to school. Luckily, the store was not very big, and her Mommy found her quickly. So they bought the juice and continued on to school.

*If the Little Girl and the Mommy feel comfortable doing it, let them hold hands as they walk around the room. Otherwise, they can just walk next to one another. As you continue the narration, the Mommy will repeat her line after you. Then the Little Girl should wander away. Once she realizes she's lost, let her look around for a moment before saying, "Oh no!" As you narrate, the Mommy will find the Little Girl and they will buy the juice and continue on to school.*

When they got there, her Mommy said, "Good-bye," and went off to work. The Little Girl spent the whole day playing with her friends. When lunchtime came, she was very glad. Remember, the Little Girl had forgotten to eat breakfast that morning, and she was getting very, very hungry.

*Let the Mommy say good-bye and return to her seat. Then call all the Friends to the space and let them play together for a few moments. As you narrate how hungry the Little Girl is, make sure the Little Girl puts on her hungry face.*

The Teacher said, "Go get your lunch boxes and sit at the table." all the kids did as she said, except for the Little Girl. She could not find her lunch box. Her friends came over to help her search, but it was not there. The Little Girl suddenly remembered that her Mommy had told her to take her lunch box. She said, "Oh no. I forgot it at home." She started to cry and the Little Girl's Teacher came over.

*Call the Teacher to the space and have her repeat her line. Once she does this, all the children should get their imaginary lunch boxes and sit down in the center of the room as though they were at a table. When the Little Girl cannot find hers, her friends can come over and help. You can stretch this out and add some fun to it by really looking all over the room for the lunch box — under chairs, behind doors. Have the Little Girl repeat her line after you and pretend to cry.*

The Teacher said, "You have not been paying attention today and that is not OK." The Little Girl knew that this was true. Her Teacher continued, "If you do not pay attention, things like forgetting your lunch box happen." For now, the Little Girl's Teacher allowed the other children, who had obeyed their parents that morning by bringing their lunches to school, to share their food with the Little Girl. But next time she had to obey her Mommy. The Little Girl promised that she would and went to her seat for lunch.

*The Teacher should come over to the Little Girl and repeat her lines after you. Remember to break up the longer ones so that she will not have to remember too much at one time. When the other children share with the Little Girl, make sure she puts on her excited face. Then give the children a second to gobble up their food. After they've done this, they can return to their seats along with the Teacher.*

At the end of the day, the Little Girl's Mommy came to pick her up from school. The Little Girl hugged her Mommy and said, "I'm sorry I didn't pay attention today. I'll follow the rules from now on." Her Mommy was glad. They went home and had a big dinner. And that night, when her Mommy told her it was time for bed, the Little Girl obeyed and climbed into bed right away.

*As the Mommy comes to the space, have the Little Girl run over to her (the hug is optional, depending on how comfortable your students feel about it). Then the Little Girl will repeat her line. Have the Mommy and the Little Girl walk around the space in a circle to signify that they are walking home. As you narrate, they will sit down and gobble up a big dinner. Then the Little Girl should lie down and go to sleep, while the Mommy returns to her seat to listen to the conclusion.*

And from then on, she obeyed her parents whenever they spoke to her. The end.

Everyone stand up and take a big giant bow.

## FOLLOW-UP ACTIVITIES

### When Should the Students Pay Attention? In this story, we learned about a Little Girl who did not pay attention to the things her Mommy told her. Is this OK? Why is it important to pay attention when grown-ups are talking? Discuss this with your students. Begin a dialogue with them about why it's important to listen and when it's important to listen. Let them offer up examples, no matter how simple or complex they are. As long as they find these things to be important, they should be paid attention to.

Call each child up to the performing space. Ask each student to tell you of a time when he or she could pay attention better. Once they have given their answer, send them back to their seat and congratulate them on knowing when it's important to pay attention to grown-ups.

### Listening Signals. It's important to pay attention in school. How can the teachers get the students to pay attention? Most likely, you are well aware of how difficult it can be to get an entire classroom of children to pay attention — especially with this age group. In many schools, a signal is created to let the students know that it's time to give the teachers their full attention. Talk about this with your students and explain the importance of a signal like this.

It's time to practice an attention signal. If you have one, take this opportunity to practice it with them. If you don't have one, it's time to create it. You will show the students this signal and tell them that when they see or hear this signal, it means that it's time to open their ears and close their mouths. It's time to pay attention to the teacher. Once you've taught this new signal to them, try it out. Call all the students to the space and let them run around and play. Then do your signal and have them quiet down. Once they get the hang of it, you can begin to make a game out of it by repeating it over and over, like freeze-dance. If you need help thinking of a signal, choose from the ones listed below:

- Turn the lights on and off two times.

- Put your hand up in the air and one finger up to your lips.

- Choose a word and say it out loud three times.

- Make a clapping pattern. When you clap it, the children repeat the pattern back to you.

**Simon Says.** It's important to listen carefully to things. Give your students examples of why it's important not just to listen but also to listen carefully. Then it's time for the ultimate listening game: Simon Says! Have all your students stand facing you in the space and explain to them how Simon Says works. You will be giving them actions to do. When the action is preceded by the words *Simon says,* then the children should do the activity. However, when the directions are not preceded by *Simon says,* the children should stand still. You can use daily activities, such as: tie your shoe, brush your teeth, comb your hair, and so on. Play a couple of rounds and encourage them to really listen to your directions. At the end, be sure to reward them for their marvelous listening skills.

# The Name Callers

## OBJECTIVES

- To teach students why name-calling is not OK
- To encourage students to be kind to others

## ROLES FOR STUDENTS TO CHOOSE FROM

| Role | Selling Point for the Students |
| --- | --- |
| Birds | Get to call people names |
| Monkeys | Get to climb trees |
| Lions | Get to act fierce and roar |
| Owls | Get to act like teachers |

## STORY SYNOPSIS

In a big, big forest there lived some Birds that liked to go on journeys. One day they decided to go on a journey to the Mystical Mountain. On their way, they stopped to ask the Monkeys to come with them. But, when the Monkeys said no, the Birds called them babies. The Birds also stopped to ask the Lions how to get there. But, when the Lions told them that they didn't know the way, the Birds called them stupid. After their trip to the Mystical Mountain, the Birds wanted to tell their friends all about their journey. But the Lions just roared at them, and the Monkeys ignored them. Finally a Wise Owl told the Birds that they should apologize to their friends for calling them names because no one likes to be called mean names. The Birds went back to their friends to apologize, and the Monkeys and Lions gave them another chance. They played and played, and the Birds decided that it was much more fun to be nice to friends.

## NARRATOR

Once upon a time, in a big, big forest, there lived some Birds. They loved to fly around and they loved to go on journeys. They also loved to call the other animals mean names. One day the Birds were playing together when _____ said, "Let's go on a journey to the Mystical Mountain." The other Birds thought that this was a great idea, and they all said, "Tweet, tweet" to show how excited they were. So off they flew.

*Call all your Birds to the performing space and let them fly around the room a few times. After all, flying was probably a big incentive in their role selection. Then insert one of the bird's names into the blank space in the story. This will prompt that child to repeat the line after you. The rest of the Birds will respond by flapping their wings and chirping, as you narrate it. Then let them continue their flight.*

They flew through the forest for a bit and decided to invite their friends, the Monkeys. They stopped by the Monkeys' trees. There, the Birds saw their friends hopping about and swinging on vines. When the Monkeys saw the Birds, they came down and said, "Hello, Birds." The Birds said, "We're going on a journey to the Mystical Mountain. Would you like to come?" The Monkeys had heard about the scary Mystical Mountain before. They had heard that there were monsters up there. And besides, the mommy monkeys had told them never to go there. So, the Monkeys all said, "No thank you. That place is too scary." The Birds were very upset that the Monkeys would not come with them. They said, "You're a bunch of babies," and they flew off.

*Call all your Monkeys to the performing space, and give them a moment to climb some trees and swing on vines. The Birds can continue flying while this goes on, or if you prefer a little less commotion, you can have them stand off to the side as they watch the Monkeys. As you narrate, the Monkeys and Birds will repeat their lines of dialogue. Have the Birds put on their angry faces and say their meanest line of all. The Monkeys can then return to their seats.*

Next, they stopped by the rock where the Lions live. The Lions were very busy running around and roaring. But, when they saw the Birds, the Lions stopped what they were doing and came over to see them. They said, "Hello, Birds." The Birds said, "We're going on a journey to the Mystical Mountain. Do you know how to get there?" The Lions talked about it with one another, but none of them could remember the way. So they said, "Sorry, but we don't know." Well, the Birds were very upset that the Lions could not help them. They said, "You guys are so stupid," and they flew off.

*Call all your Lions to the performing space and let them romp around and roar. If you notice that they associate the roaring with fighting, gently remind them that roaring is simply how Lions talk to one another. As you narrate, the Lions will walk over to the Birds and greet them. The Lions and Birds will continue their dialogue as you narrate it. Make sure the Birds put on their angry faces again before saying their meanest line of all. Then they will fly off. The Lions can return to their seats.*

Eventually the Birds made it to the Mystical Mountain, and it was just as beautiful as they had hoped. It was shiny and covered in sparkles. They flew around and around it until it was time to go home. On their way home, the Birds decided to tell their friends about their wonderful experience.

*Give the Birds a few moments to fly around the Mystical Mountain as they check it out. You may wish to let them call out things that they see there.*

They stopped by the Lions' rock once more and they said, "Lions, Lions, you'll never guess what we saw!" When the Lions saw those mean, name-calling Birds, they came over and roared at them. This scared the Birds, so they flew away quickly.

*Have the Lions come into the performing space again. As the Birds repeat their line, the Lions should roar at them as loudly as they can. The Birds will put on their frightened faces and fly away as the Lions return to their seats.*

They flew all the way to the Monkeys' trees and said, "Monkeys, Monkeys, we went to the Mystical Mountain!" But, when the Monkeys saw them, they just continued swinging on their vines and ignored the Birds.

*Have the Monkeys come into the performing space again and play in the trees as they did before. When the Birds say their line, the Monkeys can continue playing and ignore them, or they can even make mean faces at the Birds. When this section is finished, the Monkeys can return to their seats.*

The Birds did not understand why their friends wouldn't talk to them. They flew off to a tree and started to cry. Just then, an Owl sat down next to them and said, "If you call your friends names, they will not want to play with you." And the Birds said, "What should we do?" The Owl thought about it and told the Birds, "You must apologize. No one likes being called bad names." The Birds thanked the Owl and flew off to their friends.

*The Birds should sit down all together in the center of the room and start to cry. Some of them may think this is funny, and that is to be expected. After all, this is very dramatic and a little silly. The Owl will come into the space as he hears his part introduced. Let him sit down next to the Birds. The Birds and Owl will repeat their lines after you. The Birds should thank the Owl and fly away. The Owl can return to his seat.*

The Monkeys and the Lions were playing together when the Birds arrived. The Birds said, "We're sorry we called you names. We will not do that anymore." The Lions thought about it, and the Monkeys thought about it. They decided to give their friends another chance, and they all said, "OK." And they all ran off to play together.

*Once more, have the Monkeys and Lions come to the performing space where they can play together. The Birds will arrive and get their attention with their chirps and then repeat their lines of apology. The Lions and Monkeys can take their time to think about the apology, they can even scratch their heads, and then forgive the Birds. Let all the animals romp around the room together to wind down the story.*

At the end of the day, the Lions went to sleep on their rock, the Monkeys went to sleep in their trees, and the Birds flew home to their nests. The Birds decided that it was much more fun to be nice to their friends.

*Finally, let the Lions lie down in one section of the room, the Monkeys in another section, and the Birds in their own space.*

And they lived happily ever after. The end.

Everyone stand up and take a big giant bow.

## FOLLOW-UP ACTIVITIES

**Name-Calling Continued.** In this story, the birds did something that is not OK: They called their friends mean names. Why did they do this? What could they have done instead? Discuss this with your students. Ask them why they think the birds called their friends mean names. Perhaps it was because they were angry. Ask them what they think the birds should have done instead. Should they have flown away? What are some nicer words they could have used?

Call each student up to the performing space. Ask that child what he or she should say if someone makes him or her angry. You can give each child a different scenario if you wish. For example, you may ask one student what he should say if someone refuses to share with him, or ask another student what she should say or do if someone calls her a name. The point is to get your students to use their words in a positive way.

**Using Words in a Nice Way.** There are many words that people can use. Some of them can really hurt another person's feelings while others can make a friend feel really good. Discuss this with your students. Ask them for examples of words that hurt and then for examples of words that feel good. Take a moment to discuss what will happen if they continually use words that hurt. Use the birds from the story as an example. When they used hurtful words over and over, their friends didn't want to play with them anymore.

Then sit in a circle with your students. It's time to practice using words that feel good. Go around the circle and have each student say something nice to the child that is sitting next to him or her. Do this one at a time, so that the entire class listens to each other. When you have finished, have the class give a giant high-five in the center of the circle to congratulate them on using nice words.

# The Jumping Bean

## OBJECTIVES

- To teach students the importance of food
- To discuss individual likes and dislikes
- To begin a dialogue about things that are not OK to eat

## ROLES FOR STUDENTS TO CHOOSE FROM

| Role | Selling Point for the Students |
|---|---|
| Little Boy or Little Girl | Gets to jump around and be silly |
| Friends | Gets to play |
| Teacher | Gets to make the rules and act like a teacher |
| Magician | Practices magic and gives advice |

The lead role can be either a Little Boy or a Little Girl. In this lesson, it's written for a Little Boy. However, if one of the girls in your class would like to play the part, you may change the role to a Girl's, or just have her play the role as a Boy.

## STORY SYNOPSIS

There was a Little Boy who never ate his lunch. One day he found a shiny bean on the floor, which looked like much more fun to eat than his own lunch. So he put it in his mouth and ate it. Soon his body began to feel very different. It was jiggling and wiggling, and he couldn't stop bouncing. But the Boy tried to go on with his day. He tried to do a puzzle, but the pieces flew all over the place. He tried to play with his Friends, but he knocked over their block building with all of his bouncing. And he got sent out of reading class because he couldn't sit still. Just when he was beginning to think his situation was hopeless, the boy met a Magician who told him that what he had eaten was actually a jumping bean. The only way to stop the spell was to eat all the food in his lunch box. The boy quickly did this and returned to normal. He decided that from that day on, he would eat everything in his lunch box and nothing that he found on the ground.

# NARRATOR

Once upon a time Little Boy was playing with his friends at school. They were in the middle of running around when the Teacher announced that it was lunchtime. The children ran to get their lunch boxes, and they sat down at the lunch table. All the kids opened their lunches and began to eat, except for the Little Boy. He didn't like to eat his food. He wanted something more fun to eat.

*Call the Little Boy to the space, followed by the Friends. Give them a moment to run around the room together to establish the setting. Then have the Teacher come to the performing space and announce, "Lunchtime!" Point to where the students will get their lunch boxes, and the students will run to retrieve them as you narrate it. Then send them back to their seats to eat their lunches. That way, they can focus more of their attention on the actions that happen next.*

So while all the good little children ate their yummy lunches, the Little Boy wandered away from the lunch table. All of a sudden, he saw something on the ground. He looked closer and closer and closer. He saw that it was a shiny bean. This looked like fun to him, so he picked it up and ate it.

*Have the Little Boy begin to wander through the space. As you narrate, he will see the bean, pick it up, and eat it.*

As soon as he ate the bean, the Little Boy felt something mysterious and strange happening to him. Soon his belly began to jiggle and jump. Next his arms and then his legs started to wiggle and bounce. And finally his whole body began to jump up and down. He tried to ignore it and go on with his day.

*As you narrate, you may have to do the jumping with him. Your students will enjoy watching you go through the actions, too. By the end, the Little Boy's body should be jumping and shaking.*

The Little Boy tried to do a puzzle, but his body was jumping around so much that he couldn't possibly put the pieces in their places. Pieces were flying everywhere.

*Have the Little Boy stand and try to put the pieces of an imaginary puzzle together. Be sure to remind him that his body should still be jumping. You may have to continue to do that throughout the remainder of the story. As the Little Boy tries to do the puzzle, it's always fun to see him throw the pretend puzzle pieces every which way.*

So the Little Boy looked for his friends. They were busy building a tall castle with some wooden blocks. They were working very hard and had almost finished when the Little Boy walked over to play with them. But he jumped so much that he accidentally knocked the castle over and the blocks came tumbling down. The children, who had worked very hard, were angry. The Little Boy tried to explain, but they all walked away.

*Have the Friends return to the performing space and sit down in the center. Let them work for a moment on their imaginary castle. Then, as you narrate, the Little Boy should bounce his way over, still jumping around from head to toe. There's no need for him to actually topple into the group of children to show how he knocked the castle down. Your narration will serve this purpose in a safe way. Once the children learn that their castle has been knocked over, have them put on their angry faces and walk away to another part of the space.*

In reading class, the Teacher sat down with a book that all the children loved. She tried to read it aloud to them, but she was very distracted by the Little Boy. He couldn't sit still. His body was jumping about all over the place, and he was bumping into other children and generally making the room a mess. The Teacher sent him out of the room to sit alone until he could calm down. But, even outside, he couldn't sit still. He had to get some help.

*Call the Teacher to the space and have her sit down with the Friends for their reading time. The Little Boy should also go over and sit down with them. But, as his body jumps around he can gently bump into the children sitting around him. However, monitor this action closely. If you see it getting out of hand, simply remind your students that this is pretend and no one should get hurt. After a bit of the commotion, have your Teacher point to the other side of the space. As you narrate, the Little Boy will sadly go and sit there by himself, his body still jumping around, of course. Then have the Teacher and the Friends return to their seats.*

All of a sudden, the Little Boy saw a Magician looking around on the ground for something. The magician looked over at the Little Boy and saw that his body was jumping around. He approached the Little Boy and said, "Excuse me. Did you see a Jumping Bean around here?" The Little Boy was shocked to hear what he had actually eaten. "A Jumping Bean!" he said in amazement. Then, embarrassed for having eaten it, the Little Boy nodded his head yes and pointed to his stomach. "I think I ate your bean," he said. The Magician said, "Oh no!" He looked in his magician's book to find the cure for the Little Boy's jumping. When he found it, he said, "Aha! You must eat all the food in your lunch box. That will stop the jumping."

*Call the Magician to the performing space and give him a moment to look around on the ground. Then, as you narrate, the Magician and the Little Boy will repeat their lines after you. Be sure to break up the lines in this section into small chunks so that your students do not need to remember too much at one time.*

The Little Boy was so happy to hear the cure that he jumped up and ran to his lunch box. He thanked the Magician, and the Magician disappeared. The Little Boy opened up his lunch box and began to eat his sandwich, his yogurt, his apple, and his cookie. He even sipped up the juice in his juice box. Then, all of a sudden, his body stopped jumping! The Little Boy said, "Phew."

*Have the Little Boy hop and jump over to his lunch box. He should thank the Magician as he's doing this. Then the Magician will disappear back to his seat to hear the conclusion of the story.*

*In the meantime, the Little Boy will follow your narration and open up his lunch box. He will gobble up all his food ravenously. Remember to remind him that his body should still be jiggling around a bit. Then, as you narrate, he can stop the jumping. You may want to jump with him in the final moments of this and then stop abruptly as he does. Undoubtedly, he will be a bit tired of jumping at this point. Your added energy will simply help to tell the story. Once he's stopped jumping, he will sigh a relieved, "Phew."*

The Little Boy decided that from that day on, he would eat anything that was in his lunch box and nothing that he found on the ground. And he lived happily ever after. The end.

Everyone stand up and take a big giant bow.

## FOLLOW-UP ACTIVITIES

Lunch Box Food. Sometimes there are things in a student's lunch box that he or she likes and sometimes there are things that he or she doesn't like. Discuss this with your students. You can put it in terms of the story, or you can base it on each student's own experiences. Take a moment to explain to them that it's OK to have these opinions as long as they try everything once.

Call each student up to the performing space. Ask each child to tell the class his or her favorite lunchtime food. You can also ask them to tell you what food they like the least. Then pull their favorite food out of your enormous imaginary lunch box and let them gobble it up before returning to their seats. This activity will encourage your students to express their likes and dislikes while standing in front of their peers.

The Importance of Food. In this story, the Little Boy does not eat the food in his lunch box at lunchtime. Is this OK? Why not? Pose these questions to your students. Ask them why it's important to eat their food every day. What does food do for people? Encourage them to realize that food helps a person to grow and gives people energy. It affects how people move around.

Then, call all your students to the performing space to find out how certain foods will affect them. You will be calling out different foods and circumstances that will affect the way they walk around the room. First, let them walk around as they normally would. Then, call out "crackers." They will eat the pretend crackers and should take tiny steps (because they've had a little to eat). Then call out "spaghetti and meatballs" and coach them to make their steps faster because they have energy. Continue this activity with cookies, vegetables, and nothing to eat. Their footsteps can get faster and slower, smaller and larger. The idea is to have the good things make their steps fast and big while junk food and empty stomachs make their steps slow and small. This activity will help to show your students the importance of eating their food.

**Things That Are Not OK to Eat.** In this story, the Little Boy does something that is not OK: He picks up something from the ground and eats it. Talk to your students about why this is not good. They will probably tell you that the bean was dirty because it was on the ground. That's OK, but you want to emphasize that the Little Boy did not know what the bean was and they should never eat anything when they don't know what it is.

Sit in a circle with your students. You are going to discuss some things that are not OK to eat. You may want to go around the circle and ask each child to suggest something that he or she knows you shouldn't eat. Once everyone has had a turn, you will enter a more serious discussion. Talk to your students about why some things are not meant to be eaten. For example, you should discuss pills that they find in the bathroom or cleaners that they find under the sink. There's no need to scare your students. They simply need to know why these things are not good for them and that they will get sick if they eat them. No one likes a bellyache, and that's as far as you need to take it with your students.

When you have finished this discussion, be sure to end it on a positive note. Go around the circle once more and ask the students to tell you what they will eat when they go home.

# The Duck and the Pond

## OBJECTIVES

- To encourage students to accept change

- To confront some of the students' fears

## ROLES FOR STUDENTS TO CHOOSE FROM

| Role | Selling Point for the Students |
|---|---|
| Duck | Gets to swim around |
| Mommy or Daddy Duck | Gets to act like a mommy or daddy |
| Duck Friends | Get to swim around and play |
| Swan | Get to act beautiful and wise |
| An Octopus | Get to act wriggly and a little scary |

In this story, you can give your students the option of playing either a Mommy or Daddy Duck. The lesson plan is written for a Mommy, so if you have students who are interested in playing a Daddy, change the story accordingly.

## STORY SYNOPSIS

There once was a little Duck that lived in a pond. He had many Duck Friends there and loved to play with them. One day the Duck's Mommy told him that he was getting too big to live in the pond. Soon they would be moving to a lake. The Duck was very sad and very angry. He swam to the middle of the lake and cried. Soon a beautiful Swan visited him. He told the Swan that he did not want to leave his Duck Friends and that he was scared of the Octopus that was rumored to live in the lake. The Swan knew the Octopus was nice and told the Duck that he should go and see his Friends. When the Duck did this, he learned that his Friends were moving to the lake, too. When they got to the lake, the Ducks made new friends, met the nice Octopus, and learned that moving from the pond to the lake was no big deal at all.

# NARRATOR

Once upon a time there was a pond in the middle of the forest. In that pond lived a little Duck. The Duck loved living in this pond. He had many Friends, and all day long he and his friends would swim around the pond together. They would play hide and seek by hiding their heads in the water. They would swim around and play tag. And, at the end of each day, they would each go home and go to sleep.

> *Call your Duck to the performing space and let him swim around for a moment. Then call the Duck Friends to the space and let them follow along with the games in the narration. As they return home at the end of the day, the children can return to their seats.*

One day the little Duck was getting ready to go out and play when his Mommy came to see him. She said, "Little Duck, you're getting too big to live in the pond. It's time for us to move to the lake." The little Duck was very scared. He did not want to go to the big lake. He didn't know anyone there, and he had heard that there was a big scary Octopus that lived there. So, he said, "No, no, no! I don't want to live in the lake." And the little Duck swam away as fast as he could.

> *The Duck should come back to the performing space and start to get ready to go out and play. It might be fun to give him a moment to see what he does to get ready. Maybe he puts on clothes or flaps his wings. The Mommy Duck will come to the space when she hears her character announced. Have her repeat her line after you. The little Duck should put on his scared face as he repeats his line after you. Then, as you narrate, he will swim away to another part of the room. The Mommy Duck can return to her seat.*

The Duck swam to the middle of the pond and began to cry. Just then, a beautiful Swan came swimming over to where the Duck was. The Swan was wise, and she understood at once why the Duck was crying. She said, "The lake is a beautiful place to live." But the Duck was angry. He said, "What about my Friends and the scary Octopus?" The Swan just laughed. She knew the Octopus and told the Duck how nice the Octopus was. The Duck thought about this, but he wasn't sure that he should believe her. Then the Swan told the Duck to go and see his Friends and she swam off.

> *As you narrate, the Duck will sit down and cry. You may need to do this with him to take some of the pressure off. Call the Swan to the performing space and have her swim over to the Duck. She will repeat her line after you. The Duck will put on his angry face as he repeats his line. You may wish to narrate the story as written, or you can add another line or two for the Swan to tell the Duck about the Octopus and to advise him to see his Friends. Then the Swan will return to her seat.*

So the Duck went to see his Friends. They were in another part of the pond. But they weren't playing. They were sitting and talking. The Duck swam over to them and told them his news.

He said, "Friends, friends, I have to move to the lake!" His Friends all looked at him and said, "We do, too!" The Duck couldn't believe it. They were all so excited that they jumped up and down and flapped their wings. Now they could go together.

*Call the Friends to the space and have them sit down in the center of the room. The Duck will swim over to them and repeat his line after you. Then the Friends will happily say their line as well. They will all jump up and down and flap their wings as you narrate it.*

Later that day, the Duck, his Mommy, and his Friends all stepped out of the pond and waddled over to the big lake. The ducks were not sure about stepping into the lake, but once they saw the little Duck's Mommy do it, they all decided to follow her. And it wasn't that bad. That day they met other ducks that lived in the lake who were very nice to play with. There were also fish in this lake, and they made great playmates.

*Call the Mommy to the space as well. Then lead them from the pond to the lake by walking to the opposite side of the space. The ducks can all put on their scared faces right before stepping into the lake. Then, as you narrate, the Mommy should step in first, followed by the tentative steps of the other ducks. Give them all a moment to swim around and find out that it's not that bad. As you narrate the new friends, you can simply let the ducks swim around together as though they are meeting these new friends. (You can also have some of your students play the new duck friends and the fish. They are not included in the character breakdown because the roles are so small.)*

Later that week the Duck Friends met the animal that they feared most: the Octopus. He swam over to them and said, "Hi, I'm the Octopus. Want to play?" And the ducks learned that he was a nice octopus.

*Call the Octopus to the space. At first it may be fun for him to put on a mean face. This will play up the illusion in the student's minds for a moment. However, when he swims over and hears his line, he will automatically repeat it in a friendly tone. Let them all swim around together as you tell the conclusion to the story.*

Every day after that, the little Duck played with his old friends and his new friends. And before long, he learned that moving from the pond to the lake was no big deal at all. And he lived happily ever after. The end.

Everyone stand up and take a big giant bow.

## FOLLOW-UP ACTIVITIES

Finding Fears. In this story, the Duck is very scared about moving to the big lake. He's heard about the Octopus and he's afraid of it. What are the students afraid of? Discuss this with your students. First put it in terms of the story. Talk about how the Duck's fear of the

Octopus was unnecessary. Then talk to your students about their own fears. You can give some examples or ask them for some. Your students may be afraid of the dark, of the basement, of clowns, of spiders. As you discuss these things, remind your students that sometimes they don't really need to be afraid of these things, just like the Duck didn't need to be afraid of the Octopus.

Sit in a circle with your students. Go around the circle and ask each child to tell the class something that he or she is afraid of. Take a moment with each student and let him or her know that it's OK to be scared sometimes. But also remind the students that sometimes there's nothing to be afraid of at all. Most important, honor these fears without belittling them. Children need to feel that they are not foolish for feeling this way. The way to help them overcome their fears is by letting the students talk about their fears and helping them to learn that their friends feel the same way, too.

**Living with Change.** In this story, the Duck did not want to change where he lived or who his friends were. Is change bad? What's good about it? Pose these questions to your students. Put them in terms that they will understand. Children of this age are constantly going through changes, such as moving on to kindergarten, potty training, moving to a new house, or getting a new sibling. Encourage them to understand the positive sides to each of these changes.

Call each student up to the performing space. Ask each child to tell the class one change that he or she is excited about. This activity is designed to take an optimistic look at all the changes that surround a preschool student.

**The Change Machine.** One change that everyone goes through is growing up. Growing up can be fun! Take a moment to discuss this with your students. Remind them that even though it takes a long time to grow up, there are always good things about getting older and bigger.

It's time to make a Change Machine and find out what can make growing up so much fun. Have all your students come to the performing space and stand in a straight line, one behind the other. Then have them spread their legs as far as they can, while ensuring that they are comfortable and will not fall over. Tell your students that they have just made a Change Machine. When they go through the Change Machine, they will change into a big kid. One by one, starting with the student at the front of the line, the children will crawl through the tunnel of legs that is behind them. When they come out the other side, they will rejoin the line again, but this time they are big kids. Once everyone has gone through, let the class walk around the room as big kids. Sit down with your students and ask each of these big kids to tell the class one thing that is great about being big.

You can reverse this imaginary aging process by having them go through the change machine again, or you can simply have the students unzip their big-kid suits and step out of them to become themselves again.

# The Grabbing Bear

## OBJECTIVES

- To teach students why they should not grab things that don't belong to them

- To encourage students to use their words to get what they want

## ROLES FOR STUDENTS TO CHOOSE FROM

| Role | Selling Point for the Students |
|---|---|
| Little Bear | Grabs things |
| Rabbits | Gets to bounce around |
| Snakes | Slithers and hisses |
| Monkeys | Climbs trees |
| Mama Bear | Gets to act like a mommy |

If your students want to be animals that aren't listed, feel free to indulge them and use those animals in place of the characters listed above.

## STORY SYNOPSIS

There was a Little Bear who lived in a big forest and loved to play with his friends the Rabbits, the Snakes, and the Monkeys. One day he was playing with the Rabbits, and he grabbed their carrots away because he wanted them. The Rabbits did not like the way the Little Bear was playing, so they hopped away. Then, as the Little Bear was playing with the Snakes, he grabbed away a rock that the Snakes were sitting on because he wanted to sit on it. The Snakes slithered away and did not want to play with the Little Bear. And, while he was playing with the Monkeys, the Little Bear grabbed their vines away because he wanted to swing on them. So the angry Monkeys went home. When the Little Bear went home and told his Mama, she told him that he needed to use his words when he wanted something. So the next day, the Little Bear went to play with his friends who were busy building a castle out of sticks. He used his words and asked if he could use a stick, too, which his friends gladly gave him. He learned that using words worked. And every day after that, they built and played together. Whenever the Little Bear wanted to use something, he used his words first and didn't grab.

# NARRATOR

Once upon a time Little Bear lived in a big forest. He had many friends and he loved to play with them. He loved to chase his friends the Rabbits as they hopped along. He got down low and crawled around on the ground to slither like his friends the Snakes. And he loved to pretend that he could climb as high up in the trees as his friends the Monkeys. At the end of the day, they'd all go home to their mommies and daddies and go to sleep.

*Call the Little Bear to the performing space and let him skip around the room for a moment before calling the others. Then, as each set of animals is announced, let them come to the space and play with the Bear for a moment before returning to their seats. As you narrate the Bear's bedtime, he should return to his seat as well.*

But lately, the Little Bear was having a big problem — a grabbing problem. Here's what happened: One day, the Little Bear left home to go and play with his friends. First, he walked over to the Rabbits' home and asked the Rabbits to come out and play. They were all playing together when, all of a sudden, the Little Bear reached out and grabbed some carrots away from the Rabbits. The Rabbits were angry, and they said, "Hey, those are ours!" But the Bear simply ate them and said, "Well, I wanted them, too." The Rabbits did not like the way that the Bear was playing, so they hopped away and went home. The Little Bear didn't understand.

*The Bear and the Rabbits will come to the space again. Let them all romp around the room together for a moment. Then, as you narrate, the Little Bear will pretend to grab a carrot away from the Rabbits. The Rabbits will repeat their lines after you, and the Bear will follow with his line. Let the Rabbits hop angrily back to their seats.*

Next the Little Bear walked on over to the Snakes' house. He asked the Snakes to come out and play. They were slithering around when, all of a sudden, the Little Bear reached out and grabbed a rock that the Snakes had been sitting on. The Snakes did not like this, and they said, "Hey, that was our rock! We had it first." But the bear just took it and sat on it. He said, "Well, I wanted to sit on it, too. It's mine now." The Snakes did not like the way that the Little Bear was playing, and they hissed at him as they slithered home. Again, the Little Bear didn't understand.

*Call the Snakes to the performing space. Have the Bear walk over to them as he asks them to come out and play. Let this group play in the space for a moment. Then, as you narrate, the Little Bear will pretend to grab the rock from the Snakes. The Snakes and the Bear will repeat their lines as you narrate them. Once they do, make sure the Snakes give a big hiss of anger as they slither back to their seats.*

Next the Little Bear went to the Monkeys' trees and asked them to come out and play. He was swinging on some vines with them when, all of a sudden, he reached out and grabbed a vine away from the Monkeys. They were angry and said, "Hey, that was our vine!" The Little Bear shrugged and said, "Well, I wanted to swing on it, too." And he did. The Monkeys did not like the way that the Little Bear was playing, so they grabbed some new vines and swung back to their homes. But, the Bear really didn't understand.

*Have the Monkeys come to the performing space. The Bear will walk over to them and ask them if they want to come out and play. Again, give the group a moment to have fun. Once more, as you narrate, the Bear will grab the vines from the Monkeys. Both will repeat their lines after you. Then the Monkeys can swing on their vines all the way back to their seats.*

Why didn't his friends want to play with him? He walked home sadly and saw his Mama Bear. She could see that he was sad and said, "What's wrong, Little Bear?" So the Little Bear told Mama Bear the story of his day. Mama Bear shook her head and said, "Tsk, tsk, tsk. You have to use your words when you want something." The Little Bear suddenly remembered that he hadn't used his words that day. He had only used his hands to grab things. "Oh," he said. "That's why my friends won't play with me." And with that, he ran off to find his friends.

*Give the Bear a moment to circle the room as though he were walking home. Make sure he has on the saddest face he can possibly make. Then, as you narrate, Mama Bear will come to the performing space and repeat her lines after you. She's got a lot to say, so make sure to break up her lines into small chunks so that your student will not have to remember too much at one time. Little Bear will say his line and then run off to his friends. Mama Bear can return to her seat.*

The Rabbits, Snakes, and Monkeys were all playing together when the Little Bear found them. He carefully walked over to where they were building a castle out of sticks. He wanted to help, so instead of grabbing the sticks away from his friends, the Little Bear said, "Excuse me, can I use one of those sticks?" The other animals were surprised that the Little Bear wasn't grabbing. They all offered him some sticks to build with, and the Little Bear could tell that using his words was already working.

*All the animals will come to the space when they hear their roles called again. Have them sit down in the center and pretend to build their stick castle. Little Bear will approach them and kindly repeat his line. Let the other students hand him as many sticks as they like. This is a great reward to give the Bear for using his words so well. Let them stay in the space and continue to play as you narrate the conclusion to the story.*

And every day after that, they built and played together. Whenever the Little Bear wanted to use something, he used his words first and didn't grab. And all the animals lived happily ever after. The end.

Everyone stand up and take a big giant bow.

# FOLLOW-UP ACTIVITIES

**Using Words.** In this story, the Little Bear does something that is not OK: He grabs things away from his friends. Discuss this with your students. Ask them to tell you why it's not right to grab things that don't belong to them, and discuss the consequences of doing it. In this story, the Little Bear's friends didn't want to play with him anymore. Then ask your students to tell you what they should do if they want something that someone else has. Discuss the importance of asking nicely.

Tell your students that you have an imaginary bag full of toys. Then, call each child up to the performing space. Pull a toy out of the bag that you know that particular student would really like. Tell the child that he or she can have this toy; the child just have to use his or her words to get it. Encourage your students to use full sentences when asking for the toy (rather than just saying *please*). And make sure that the student uses his or her words *before* reaching over to grab the toy. The emphasis is on words first.

**Asking Nicely.** When asking to use something, there are nice words to use and mean words. Which do the students think are better? Discuss this with your students. Give them some examples of each. For instance, some mean words to use when a person wants something might include: "Hey, you babies, give me that toy." However, some nice words to use are: "Excuse me, can I play with that?" Talk to your students about why they should use nice words.

Sit in a circle with your students and tell them to bring the toys that they received during the last activity. Tell your students that it's time to use their words to share these toys. If someone uses nice words, everyone will clap for him or her. If someone uses mean words, everyone will stomp the ground with their feet. Go around the circle and have each student ask the child to his or her right if he or she can play with that child's toy. First, tell the student to use mean words, then nice words. And make sure the students who are watching respond with the appropriate hand clapping or foot stomping. This activity will add a bit of fun to the task of deciphering which words to use.

# UNIT 6
## New Ideas

The New Ideas unit will introduce students to a variety of new words and concepts. These range from learning what a mailman does to finding out what a veterinarian is. Some stories have specific roles for the class to choose, while others are designed to let the entire class play children like in the Adventure Stories.

Before beginning each story, use the Prestory Discussion to introduce the children to the new word or idea. The class does not need to come away from this brief dialogue with a full understanding of the new concept; the story and follow-ups will help to take care of that. However, it's helpful for the students to be familiar with the topic before diving into the lesson.

These stories teach students by capitalizing on the ability of storytelling to capture a child's attention. The students will be more interested in learning because their imaginations will be engaged.

# The Veterinarian

## OBJECTIVE

- To teach students about veterinarians

## PRESTORY DISCUSSION

Before you begin this story with your students, sit down with them and tell the students that a veterinarian is an animal doctor. Once they understand this, have them repeat the word after you a couple of times. Admittedly, this word is a pretty long one and a difficult one to say. If you feel that your students are having too much trouble saying the word, you can always shorten it to vet. However, be consistent. Whichever way you teach it, use that form for the remainder of your lesson, or your students will get confused.

## ROLES FOR STUDENTS TO CHOOSE FROM

| Role | Selling Point for the Students |
|---|---|
| Mommy and Daddy | Gets to act like a mommy or daddy |
| Dog | Gets to bark and play a lot |
| Little Boy or Little Girl | Takes good care of the dog |
| Veterinarian | Gets to act like an animal doctor |
| Nurse | Helps the veterinarian |

In this story, the child can be a boy or a girl. It makes no difference. However, for this lesson plan, the part is written as a Little Boy.

## STORY SYNOPSIS

A Little Boy had a wonderful Dog that he played with every day. One day when the Little Boy came home from school, he noticed that the Dog didn't want to play. The Little Boy thought that his Dog was probably just tired, so he left the Dog alone. But, after a few days of this, the Little Boy went to his parents to ask what he should do. His Mommy and Daddy put the Little Boy and the Dog in the car, and they all headed to the Veterinarian's office. There the Little Boy saw that all kinds of animals come to see a Veterinarian so that they can be healthy pets. When it was their turn, the Dog and his family went into a room that had a table for the Dog to jump up and sit on. The Veterinarian came in and checked the Dog out. He told the family that their Dog just had a cold. He gave them some dog medicine for him to take, and before long the Dog was feeling better. A few days later, when the Little Boy came home from school, his Dog came out to the yard to greet him. They played fetch and ran around the yard together. And the Little Boy knew then that his Dog was feeling better — thanks to the Veterinarian.

## NARRATOR

Once upon a time there was a Little Boy who had a wonderful dog. The Boy and his Dog loved to play together. Every day, when the Little Boy would get home from school, he would take his Dog outside to play. First, they would play fetch, and the Dog would chase after sticks and toys. Then, they would chase each other around the yard. The Dog and the Little Boy were best friends.

*Call the Little Boy and the Dog to the performing space and let them run around and play together. As you narrate, the Little Boy will throw imaginary sticks and toys for the Dog to chase after. You can have the Little Boy go over to the Dog and pet him. This will help to establish their close friendship. At the end of this part, have them return to their seats before beginning the next part.*

One day the Little Boy came home from school and ran to his Dog for the usual outside playtime. But the Little Boy was shocked. His Dog didn't want to come outside and play. The Dog just stayed on his bed. The Little Boy thought that his Dog must be tired, and he left the Dog alone.

*Call the Little Boy to the space again. He will run in as though he were coming home from school. You can even have him take off an imaginary backpack so he can really get into the setting and time. Then call the Dog to a corner of the space, and as you narrate, he will just lie there. The Little Boy should put on his surprised face when he sees that the Dog does not want to play. Then he can return to his seat as he leaves the tired Dog alone.*

The next day, when the Little Boy came home from school, he saw that his Dog was doing the same thing — lying on his bed again. The Little Boy thought this was strange. So he went and found his parents.

*The Little Boy will enter the space once more and walk over to the sleeping Dog. He can scratch his head to show that he thinks this is strange. Then he will walk to a different part of the space to find his parents. At this point, you may choose to let the Dog remain where he is or have him return to his seat.*

He told his parents what had happened and asked them, "Do you think he's sick?" The Little Boy's Mommy and Daddy said, "We don't know. Let's find out." So they decided to take the Dog to the Veterinarian's office.

*When they hear their characters called, the Mommy and Daddy will come to the performing space. The Little Boy and the parents will repeat their lines after you.*

Mommy, Daddy, the Little Boy, and their Dog all got into the car. They put on their seat belts and drove to the Veterinarian's office. When they walked in, the Little Boy couldn't believe what he was seeing. His Dog was not the only one there. There were other dogs, cats, rabbits, and even snakes in the waiting room. They were all there to see the Veterinarian who would make them feel better.

*Point to where the car will be so that your students know where to go. If you have previously used the car in your lessons, try to place it in the same spot as before for continuity's sake. The students will all put on their seat belts as you narrate it. It's fun for the Dog to do this, too. As they arrive at the vet's office, show them where the door will be and let them walk in. The Little Boy should put on his surprised face when he hears you narrate what other animals are there. You can have your students play the other animals in the waiting room if you wish. These roles are not included in the Roles for Students to Choose From because they are so small. But, if you've got a kid who's dying to play one of the waiting animals, by all means, let him do it.*

The Little Boy walked right up to the Nurse and said, "We're here to see the Veterinarian." The Nurse nodded and told him to have a seat while he waited.

*Call the Nurse to the performing space and the Little Boy will say his line to her. The Nurse will tell him to sit down while he waits. At this point, if you have other students playing waiting-room animals, you may wish to let these animals have a little conversation with the Dog or ask each other why they came to see the Veterinarian.*

Before long, the Nurse came out and told the Little Boy it was his turn to bring in his Dog. The Little Boy, his Dog, and his parents walked into the Veterinarian's office. There was a big table for the Dog to sit on and the Boy's Mommy and Daddy helped the Dog up.

*The Nurse will walk over to the Boy and say, "Your turn," as you narrate it. Have the Boy, Dog, and parents walk across to the other side of the performing space as they walk into the Veterinarian's office. (If other students were playing waiting-room animals, they should return to their seats.) The Mommy and Daddy should pretend to lift the Dog up onto the table. Be sure not to let them really attempt this as someone may wind up getting hurt. You may use a chair as the Dog table if you wish.*

In came the Veterinarian. The Dog barked because he knew that this doctor would help him. The Veterinarian bent down to pet the Dog and gave him a doggy treat to make him feel at home. Then he looked in the Dog's ears and down his throat. He listened to the Dog's heartbeat and then he said, "Don't worry, your Dog just has a cold." The Little Boy was very relieved. The nurse came in, gave the Boy's parents some pills for the Dog, and then it was time to go.

*Call the Veterinarian to the performing space, and he will walk over to the Dog. As you narrate, the Dog will start barking. The Vet will pet the Dog, give him some doggy treats, and check him out. Then the Veterinarian will repeat his line after you. In turn, the Little Boy should wipe his brow and say, "Phew." As she hears her part, the Nurse will come to the space again and give the parents the dog medicine. Then the Veterinarian and the Nurse can return to their seats.*

The Little Boy and his parents put the Dog back in their car, and they all drove back home. Before long, the Dog was feeling better. He had taken his doggy medicine, and now his cold was gone.

*The Boy, Dog, and parents should all return to the car, put on their seat belts, and drive away from the Veterinarian's office. Have them all get out of the car and return to their seats.*

When the Little Boy came home from school a few days later, his Dog came out to greet him. They played fetch and ran around the yard together. And the Little Boy knew then that his Dog was all better.

*Call the Little Boy to the space one last time and have him take off his backpack again as though he is coming home from school. The Dog should come to the space and greet him. Give them some time to run around together before telling the conclusion to the story.*

They were thankful that the Veterinarian had helped. And they lived happily ever after. The end.

Everyone stand up and take a big giant bow.

# FOLLOW-UP ACTIVITIES

### It's the Students' Turn to See the Vet. In this story, the Veterinarian helps animals feel better. What kinds of animals did he see? Discuss this with your students. Ask them to recall what kinds of animals were waiting to see the Veterinarian in this story. Then ask them to tell you other kinds of animals that people have as pets. Let them know that a veterinarian treats all kinds of animals when they are sick.

Let each student act like an animal of his or her choice. Tell the students that they are now waiting to see the Veterinarian. Call each student up to the performing space and into your office (you are the vet). Ask them to tell you what is wrong with him or her and why the student came to see the veterinarian, then prescribe a cure. This can range from giving a Band-Aid to giving medicine. Once the students are cured, send the children back to their seats. Make sure that all the animals get a chance to see the veterinarian before the end of the day. This activity will help to show your students that a vet treats all kinds of animals.

**Time to Be the Vet.** We've just learned about animals that go to a veterinarian's office when they are sick. What about animals that are too big to go to a doctor's office? Talk about this with your students. Ask them to tell you what they think happens when a really big animal needs to see a veterinarian, like an elephant, horse, cow, sheep, pig, or rhino. Answer this question for them (if they cannot figure out the answer for themselves) by telling them that there are some veterinarians that go to farms and zoos to see the animals. That way the big animals don't have to fit into a little office.

Tell your students that it's their turn to be the farm vets. Make sure they pack their doctors' bags and fill them up with anything they think they might need to help these big animals. Then it's time to take a ride to a farm. When you get there, show your students where the different ailing animals are. In one corner of the room you will put pigs, while another corner will be where the horse stables are. Give them as many options as you can. Then let them spread out throughout the room as they help whichever animals they wish. Give them a minute or two to let them really explore the space and put their veterinary skills to work. When they are all done, they can return to their offices and collapse for a nap. After all, it's hard work being a farm vet.

# The Mailman and the Post Office

## OBJECTIVES

- To teach students how the mail system works
- To encourage children to think of others

## PRESTORY DISCUSSION

In this story, you teach your students how the mail system works. Before you begin, you may want to take a few moments to find out how much they know and to fill them in on what they don't. First, talk about letters and why people send them. Some people send letters to say hello, while others send invitations or birthday cards. When someone writes a letter, they have to put it in an envelope. Next, tell your students that there are three things that have to go onto an envelope before the mailman will deliver it: where it's going, who it's going to, and a stamp. Take this time to talk about addresses and what they are. Some of your students will know this information already, while others will be completely confused. Don't worry if it seems like a lot for your students to handle. That is why the story is here — to help teach them this lesson. However, this prestory discussion will make sure you and your students are on the same page during the lesson. Proceed with fun!

## ROLES FOR STUDENTS TO CHOOSE FROM

| Role | Selling Point for the Students |
|---|---|
| Mommy or Daddy | Gets to act like a mommy or daddy |
| Little Boy or Little Girl | Has a birthday party, gets to send mail |
| Mailman | Delivers letters and carries the mail |
| Friends | Get to go to a party and receive letters |

In this story, the child can be a boy or a girl. It makes no difference. You will find the character written for a girl, but feel free to change it according to your student's wishes. In addition, it's perfectly acceptable if you only have one parent in the story, even though the lesson is written for two.

## STORY SYNOPSIS

A little girl was having a birthday. She went with her parents to pick out party invitations. Then she sat down and wrote the party information on the invitations. She put them in envelopes, wrote a friend's name and address on each of them, and then placed a stamp in the corner. Then the Little Girl walked out to the mailbox and put the invitations inside. The next morning, the Mailman picked the invitations up and took them to the post office to be sorted. The day after that, the Mailman went to the post office to get the mail that he had to deliver that day. He dropped off the Little Girl's invitations at each of her friend's mailboxes, and when the children got home, they were excited to see that they were invited to a party. The day of the party was great fun. There was dancing, games, a cake, and gifts. Afterward, the Little Girl sent out thank-you cards to all her friends. The Mailman delivered them, and the children remembered what a wonderful time they had had at the Little Girl's party.

## NARRATOR

Once upon a time a little girl was having a birthday. One day her Mommy and Daddy came to her room. They walked inside and told her, "It's time to plan your birthday party!" The Little Girl was very excited and said, "Hooray!"

*Call the Little Girl to the performing space and let her skip around for a moment. Then call the Mommy and Daddy to the space. They will walk toward the Little Girl and repeat their line after you. The Little Girl will put on her excited face and repeat her cheer.*

First, they went to the card store and bought some invitations. The Little Girl would be sending these to her friends to let them know where and when the party was going to be. She looked around the store very carefully and picked out the invitations that she liked the best. Her parents paid for them, and they all went home.

*Your students will follow you as you circle the room and go to the card store. Let the Little Girl look around and pick out her invitations. She will probably want to tell you what kind she picked out. It means that she has completely given herself over to the life of the story. It's also a great way for her to express a little individuality. The Mommy and Daddy can pay you, and then they will all walk back the way they came.*

That night the Little Girl's parents told her, "It's time to fill in these invitations." So, they sat down with her and began to write. On each invitation, they wrote all the information about the Little Girl's party. Then, when they were done filling in all the invitations, it was time to address the envelopes. The Little Girl wrote a friend's name on each of the envelopes, and then she wrote their address. Finally, when she was done with that, she had to put a stamp on the envelope so the mailman would deliver it. She did this with each envelope: name, address, and stamp.

*When they stop walking back from the store, the Mommy and Daddy will repeat their line. All three will sit down on the floor together. As you narrate the exposition of this section, the children who are in the story can simply sit and pretend to write. When you reach the last sentence of this section, you may want to repeat it a number of times and even have the whole class repeat it with you. It will really help to get this process into their heads.*

When they were finished, the Little Girl went outside to the mailbox and put all the invitations inside for the mailman to pick up the next day. She was very tired from all this hard work, so she went upstairs and went to bed.

*The Little Girl can walk to any part of the space and put the envelopes in the mailbox. Then the Little Girl, Mommy, and Daddy can all return to their seats as though they were going to bed.*

The next morning the Mailman was out on his route. When he got to the Little Girl's mailbox, he opened it up and saw that there were a lot of envelopes for him to pick up. He put them in his mailbag and walked to the rest of the mailboxes on his route. At the end of the day, he returned to the post office and handed in all the letters that he had collected so that they could be sorted out and brought to the right houses. The next day, when the Mailman got to the post office, he picked up the mail that he needed to deliver and left on his route again. He dropped the letters off at each of the Friend's houses and finished his delivering and collecting.

*Call the Mailman to the performing space and let him walk around on his mail route. As you narrate, he will go to the Little Girl's mailbox (roughly where she originally placed it) and take out the letters to be delivered. Let him collect some more mail from other mailboxes as well. Then he can walk to a separate part of the room to drop the letters at the post office. As you narrate, he will pick up the mail to be delivered and start to walk around the room again. To deliver the invitations, the Mailman can stop in front of each student's seat and place the invitation in individual mailboxes right in front of each student. Then the Mailman can return to his own seat.*

When the Little Girl's friends came home from school that day, they opened up their mailboxes and saw letters addressed to them. They opened the envelopes and said, "Oh boy, a party!" And what a party it was.

*The children can open their mailboxes from their seats. As you narrate, they will each open a mailbox and take out the letter. Then the Friends will repeat their line after you.*

On the day of the Little Girl's birthday party, all her friends were there. They danced, played games, and had a wonderful time. They sang "Happy Birthday" and even had some cake. Then they sat down and watched the Little Girl open her birthday presents. Finally, when the party was finished, the children said good-bye and went back to their homes.

*Have the Little Girl and all the Friends come to the performing space. You can stretch this section out as long as you wish. Put on some music and let them dance, play some games, and sing "Happy Birthday" to the Little Girl. Then let the children sit down in a circle as they eat their imaginary birthday cake. The Little Girl opening her presents creates another wonderful opportunity for some creativity. Ask each of the Friends to tell her what gift they got her. When you are ready to finish this section, have the Friends say good-bye as they return to their seats.*

The next day the Little Girl's parents came into her room and said, "Time to write thank-you notes." So the Little Girl sat down and wrote more notes to her friends, thanking them each for the birthday presents they had given her. When she was done, she put them in envelopes, wrote the names and addresses, and put on the stamps. Then she walked outside and put them in the mailbox to be delivered.

*Call the parents to the performing space. They will walk over to the Little Girl and repeat their line after you. Then they can return to their seats once more. The Little Girl will sit down and pretend to write again. You can make a big deal about the name, address, and stamp as you did the first time. She will walk to where the mailbox was the first time and put the envelopes inside. Once she's done all this, the Little Girl can return to her seat.*

That same day, the Mailman came to the Little Girl's mailbox and took out all the letters to be mailed. He took them to the post office to be sorted and then delivered them to her friends' houses.

*Call the Mailman to the space. He will pick up the letters as you narrate it and deliver the thank-you notes to each of the friends in the same way as he did before: by putting them in mailboxes directly in front of each student. When he is done with his route, the Mailman can return to his seat.*

When her friends opened their mailboxes that day, they looked at her letter and said, "Oh boy, a note for me!" They read her thank-you note and remembered what a good time they had had at the birthday party.

*From their seats, the Friends can open their mailboxes and find their letters. They will excitedly repeat their lines after you.*

As the little girl and all her friends went to sleep that night, they were glad that the mailman had delivered all their mail so that they could each have such a wonderful time. The end.

Everyone stand up and take a big giant bow.

# FOLLOW-UP ACTIVITIES

### Who Will Each Student Send a Letter To? In this story, the little girl sent invitations and thank-you notes to her friends. What else can people say in a letter? Discuss this with your students and pose this question to them. Since you have just told a story that involved birthday invitations, they will undoubtedly have this topic on the brain. Help them to expand their ideas. Let them know that people send letters to say hello, to tell someone to feel better, or just to say, "I love you."

Call each student to the performing space. Ask that child who they would send a letter to and what that letter would say. Then give the student an imaginary piece of paper and pen and let them write the letter. When they've finished, drop it in a pretend mailbox for them and have them sit down. This activity will encourage your students to think about the nice things that can be expressed to the people they love.

### Stamp Designs. In the story, the students learned that every letter needs a stamp to be delivered. Did any students know that stamps come with many different designs on them? Discuss this with your students. Take this opportunity to explain to them what kinds of designs, patterns, and pictures are on some stamps. Ask your students if they have ever seen stamps. If so, what did they look like?

Have all your students sit down in the performing space and let them spread out. Tell them that you are handing out imaginary stamps that have no designs on them. Give them imaginary markers or paints. It's time to create their own stamp designs. Tell your students that they can draw any kind of picture on these stamps. Give them a minute to really get the job done and encourage them to add as much detail as possible.

When they have finished, have each child stand up and show the class the stamp that he or she made. Let that student tell the class about his or her picture or design and again encourage the student to describe it in as much detail as possible. When all the students have had a chance, collect the imaginary stamps and tell your students that you will bring these to the mailman to see what he thinks!

### Do Any Students Know Their Own Address? In this story, the students learned that one of the things that must go on an envelope is an address, which is where someone lives. Do your students know their addresses? Sit in a circle with your students and begin a discussion about this topic. Many of your students will have no idea what their address is. Some may know what street they live on or even the number of their house. A precious few will have been taught what their entire address is.

Whatever the case, go around the circle and ask each student to tell you as much of his or her address as possible. If any students don't know any part of their addresses, you can at least tell them what state they live in. It may also be fun to encourage them to go home and find out what their address is. Even if you have only piqued their interest about finding this information, you have taught them a wonderful lesson. When each student has had a chance, have the class get into their cars and drive back to their homes.

# The Travel Agency

## OBJECTIVES

- To teach students the function of a travel agency

- To encourage children to imagine different geographical settings

- To learn about the various modes of transportation

## PRESTORY DISCUSSION

Before beginning your story, take a few moments to talk to your students about the functions of a travel agency. Let them know that a travel agency is a place where many people go to plan their vacations. A Travel Agent tells people about fun places to go, helps them decide how they want to get there (plane, train, boat), and tells them which price will be the best one. Then the agent gives her customers their tickets to go on their vacation. Although online travel booking is gradually making the travel agency obsolete, your students will benefit from planning a trip together and learning the stages of preparation that go into a vacation.

## ROLES FOR STUDENTS TO CHOOSE FROM

| Role | Selling Point for the Students |
| --- | --- |
| Duck | Gets to act like a cousin of Donald Duck |
| Cousin Duck | Gets to play in the pond |
| Fish | Gets to travel to the sea |
| Brother and Sister Fish | Get to swim around in the water |
| Little Boy or Little Girl | Travels on a train |
| Grandma and Grandpa | Get to act like grandparents |
| Travel Agent | Helps people plan their trips |

The role of the Travel Agent can be played by a student, but feel free to take the part yourself. And, as always, it's perfectly acceptable to change the role of the Little Boy to a Little Girl.

## STORY SYNOPSIS

There was a Travel Agent who had some strange visitors. One day a Duck came into her office. He wanted to take a plane to Disney World to go and see his cousin Donald. So the Travel Agent planned the trip and gave him a plane ticket. The next day a Fish came into the office. He wanted to take a boat to California to see his brothers and sisters who swam in the ocean there. So the Travel Agent planned it for him and gave him his ticket. The next day the Travel Agent was expecting some more odd visitors, but a Little Boy walked into the office. He wanted to take a train to see his grandparents. So the Travel Agent planned the trip for him and gave the Little Boy a ticket. The Duck, the Fish, and the Little Boy traveled to see their families and greeted them with quacks, swimming, and hugs. They all had a wonderful time on their vacations, and it was all thanks to the help of a nice Travel Agent.

## NARRATOR

Once upon a time there was a place where people went to plan a vacation. This place was called a Travel Agency. In this Travel Agency, there worked a person who helped people all day long. One day the Travel Agent was sitting at her desk when a Duck walked in! The Travel Agent was very surprised to see a Duck in her office. He walked over to her desk and said, "I need to plan a trip to Disney World." The Travel Agent was still pretty shocked, so she said, "Why?" The Duck told her that he had to get there to see his cousin, Donald Duck. The Travel Agent understood. So they sat down together and planned his trip.

*Call the Travel Agent to the performing space and have her sit down at her imaginary desk. You may want to use two chairs for the lesson so that your students can sit in them as they work with the Travel Agent. However, it's fine to just have them sit on the floor. The Duck will come to the space as his part is narrated. He will walk over to the Travel Agent, and they will repeat their dialogue.*

She asked him if he wanted to take a plane, and he said that he would definitely like to fly. So she gave him a plane ticket. She asked him how long he would stay there, and he told her he would be staying for a week. So she made a reservation at a lovely Pond Hotel. The Duck said, "Thank you," to the Travel Agent, and he walked out the door. The Travel Agent shook her head because she still couldn't believe that she had just planned a trip for a duck.

*Feel free to have your students engage each other in this conversation by repeating the dialogue after you. The Duck will thank her and return to his seat. After the Duck exits, give the Travel Agent a moment to keep her surprised face on.*

The next day the Travel Agent was sitting in her office, and a Fish swam in. The Travel Agent couldn't believe her eyes. The Fish swam right over to her desk and said, "I would like to go to the beach." The Travel Agent was so surprised that she had to ask, "Why?" That's when the Fish told her that he had to go visit his brothers and sisters who swam all the way to California. Now that she understood, they sat down together and planned his trip.

*Call the Fish to the performing space. He will walk over to the Travel Agent and repeat his line after you. Then you can have the Fish repeat his explanation or just make it part of your narration.*

She asked him how he would like to get there. The Fish thought about it and said that he would like to travel by water. So the Travel Agent gave him a ticket on a cruise boat. She asked him what kind of room he would like to stay in on that boat, and the Fish told her he would like a room filled with water. So she made a reservation for him. When they were done, the Fish made sure to say "thank you," and he walked out the door.

*Again, feel free to let your students engage in this dialogue. Then the Fish will thank her and return to his seat.*

The next day the Travel Agent was expecting to see some more crazy animals. So she was surprised when a Little Boy walked in the door. He walked over to her and said, "I would like to go see my Grandma and Grandpa." This the Travel Agent definitely understood. The Little Boy sat down, and they planned his trip.

*Call the Little Boy to the performing space. He will walk over to the Travel Agent and repeat his line. The Travel Agent can put on her happy face after the Little Boy explains his situation.*

The Travel Agent asked the Little Boy how he would like to get there, and the Little Boy said he would like to take a train. She asked him when he would like to come back, and the Little Boy said that the following weekend would be good. He said that he didn't need a hotel because his Grandma and Grandpa had a room all made up for him with toys and everything. So the Travel Agent gave him a train ticket. The Little Boy said, "Thank you," and he walked out the door. That night the Travel Agent went home very tired.

*Once more, let the students repeat the dialogue after you as they carry on their conversation. The Little Boy will thank her and return to his seat. Then the Travel Agent can stand up with her tired face on and return to her seat as well.*

The next day, the Duck got on an airplane, the Fish got on a boat, and the Little Boy got on a train. They traveled for hours.

*The Duck will come to the space as his character is called. Have him sit down on the floor to indicate that he has gotten on the plane. The Fish will enter the space as his character is called. Have him sit in another part of the space to indicate that he has boarded his boat. The Little Boy will come to the space as his character is called. Have him sit in yet another part of the space to indicate that he has gotten onto his train.*

When the Duck got off his plane, his cousin Donald ran to meet him. They quacked and quacked as they caught up on old times. Then Donald took the Duck to a pond and they swam around all day long. The Fish got off his boat and immediately jumped into the ocean in California. He found his brothers and sisters and they swam around all day. They showed him all the different underwater sights and had a marvelous time. And, when the Little Boy got off his train, his Grandma and Grandpa were there to give him hugs. He went to their house and played with his toys, ate cookies, and was very happy.

*As you narrate, the Duck will stand up to get off his plane. Call the Cousin Duck to the space and have him walk over to the Duck. They will quack and swim around for a moment. Then they can return to their seats. Then the Fish will stand up and jump into the water. Call the Brother and Sister Fish to the space and give them all a few moments to swim around together. They can return to their seats when they're done. Then the Little Boy will stand up to get off his train. Call the Grandma and Grandpa to the space and let them give the boy a hug (or a high-five — whatever your students feel most comfortable with). They can run around and play with his imaginary toys. Then they will return to their seats.*

They all had a wonderful time on their vacations and it was all thanks to the help of a nice Travel Agent. The end.

Everyone stand up and take a big giant bow.

## FOLLOW-UP ACTIVITIES

Vacation Time. In this story, the Duck, the Fish, and the Little Boy plan vacations in different parts of the country. Have any students been on a vacation? Discuss the idea of a vacation with your students. Let them know that one doesn't necessarily have to take a plane to go on a vacation. A person can drive a car, too. A vacation is just a trip to some place that is not home.

Call each child to the performing space. Ask that student to tell the class one place that he or she has gone on a vacation. The answers may range from Disney World to Uncle Joe's. The idea is to get the students thinking about different settings and to expand their view of the world just a little bit more.

Getting There. There are lots of ways to travel. What are some of the ways the students learned about in the story? Are there any others? Discuss this with your students. Ask them to recall how the various characters got to their vacation spots in the story. Ask your students if any of them have ever traveled on a plane, train, or boat. You may also want to take a moment to discuss why people choose to travel a certain way to a certain location. For example, a person takes a plane when something is really far away. A person takes a boat to see the ocean. Let your students also suggest some reasons why they would travel one of these ways. You might get some wonderfully creative answers.

It's time for a little travel fun! Call all your students to the performing space and let them know that it's time to experience the different ways to travel. First, board a plane. You can make this as detailed as you wish by sitting them in rows, giving them imaginary beverages, experiencing turbulence (or air bumps so it's less scary). Then, travel by train. Again, some fun additions might be to meet the conductor, let them sit backward, and so on. Or you can create a human choo-choo train and simply travel around the room together. Finally, get onto a boat. You can make it a large cruise ship, or you can make it a rowboat. Be sure to look at the dolphins jumping out of the water as you travel across the ocean. Then drive all your students back to school in a good old car.

## Where Would Each Student Like to Go? In the story, the students learned that people can travel to many different places. If each student could choose, where would he or she travel? Take a moment to let your students think about this question.

Then sit in a circle with your students. Go around the circle and ask each student to tell the class where he or she would go if he or she could travel anywhere. Once the student has made a decision, hand out a ticket and let the child zoom around the outside of the circle as he or she travels to this place. The student then returns to the circle. This activity is a great chance for your students to express their individuality and to live out some more of their traveling fantasies.

# The Architect

## OBJECTIVES

- To teach students the job of an architect
- To encourage cooperation among students

## PRESTORY DISCUSSION

Before beginning the story, take a few moments to explain to your students what an architect is. Tell them that an architect is someone who designs buildings and houses. To bring this concept closer to their reality, you may wish to use their own drawings as an example. For instance, have them imagine what it would be like if the pictures that they drew of houses and buildings actually got put together for people to live and work in. That's what an architect does: He draws pictures of buildings, and other people build them. Make sure your students repeat this new word a few times. Then you're ready for business as usual.

## ROLES FOR STUDENTS TO CHOOSE FROM

| Role | Selling Point for the Students |
|------|-------------------------------|
| Architect | Designs beautiful buildings & houses |
| Builders | Build the architect's designs |
| Horse | Gets to gallop around |
| Dog | Gets to bark and play |
| Little Boy or Little Girl | Climbs trees |

If your students are dying to play animals other than horses and dogs, feel free to add their ideas to the story. And, the role of the Little Boy can change to that of a Little Girl.

## STORY SYNOPSIS

An Architect worked in an office. He spent all day drawing pictures and designing houses for people. Lately he had begun to have some strange and unusual customers, though. One day a Horse walked into his office and asked him to build a house for his horse family. The Architect drew pictures of a beautiful stable and had his Builders build it. When the Horse saw the new stable, he galloped around to show how much he liked it. The next day a Dog came into the office and asked the Architect to design a house for him. The Architect drew some pictures of a new doghouse and had his Builders get to work. When the Dog came to see the doghouse, he barked and wagged his tail to show just how much he liked it. The next day a Little Boy came into the office and asked the Architect to build a tree house for him. Again, the Architect drew some pictures and set his builders to work. The Little Boy loved his new tree house and thought of all the fun he would have inside with his friends. That night the Horse and her family lay down in their new stables, the Dog went to sleep in his new doghouse, and the Little Boy slept in his sleeping bag inside his new tree house. And as they all went to sleep, they thanked the Architect for making such beautiful new homes for them.

## NARRATOR

Once upon a time an Architect worked in an office. He spent all day drawing pictures and designing houses for people. Lately he had begun to have some strange and unusual customers, though.

> *Call the Architect to the performing space and let him sit down in his office for a moment to establish the setting.*

One day a Horse walked into his office. The Architect was very surprised to see a Horse in his office. But the Horse walked up to the Architect and said, "Can you build me a house please?" The Architect was wondering why a Horse needed a house, so he asked, "What kind of house?" The Horse said, "I need some stables for me and my family." The Architect said he would do it. He shook the Horse's hoof and the Horse galloped out of the office.

> *Call the Horse to the performing space and have her walk up to the Architect. As you narrate, the Horse and the Architect will repeat their dialogue after you. When the Horse is finished, she will gallop back to her seat.*

The Architect quickly got to work. He sat down and drew some beautiful pictures of horse stables with rooms for the Horse's kids to play in. Then he called his Builders. The Builders looked at the drawings and started to build. They built and built and built until they had built the horse stables just as the Architect had drawn them. When they were done, they gave each other high-fives and went home.

> *Once the Horse has left the space, the Architect can sit down again and begin to draw. Give him a moment to sketch the stables out. Then call the Builders to the space. The Architect will give them the drawing. Let them look at it for a moment. Then the Builders will pretend to build this imaginary stable. Feel free to let them run around the space as they gather their building materials. When they are finished, they will give each other high-fives and return to their seats.*

Soon, the Horse came to the new stable that was specially designed and built by the Architect and his Builders. She said, "Neigh!!!" and galloped around her new home to show just how happy she was.

*Call the Horse to the performing space. Let her gallop around the space as though she is running through her new house. Make sure that she lets out a loud "neigh" to show her approval. After a moment or two of this, she can return to her seat.*

The next day the Architect was sitting in his office when a dog walked in. The Architect was very surprised to see a dog in his office. The Dog walked over to him and said, "Can you build me a house?" The Architect thought he knew what kind of house the dog wanted. So he said, "Do you want a doghouse?" The Dog barked to show that that was exactly what he wanted. He also asked for some stairs to the roof of the doghouse so that he could guard the yard better. The Architect said that he could do it. So the Architect shook the dog's paw and the dog walked out of the office.

*Call the Architect to the space, followed by the Dog. The Dog will walk over to him and the two students will repeat their dialogue after you. Then they will shake hands, and the Dog can return to his seat.*

The Architect got to work. He sat down and drew some beautiful pictures of a doghouse with a staircase. When he was done, he called in his Builders. The Builders looked at the drawings and started to build. They built and built and built until they were all done with the doghouse. When they were done, they shook hands and went back home.

*Once the Dog has left the space, the Architect can sit down and draw. Again, let him take his time. When he is finished, call the Builders to the space. They will look at the drawing and begin to build. As you narrate, they will shake hands and return to their seats.*

Soon the Dog came to his new doghouse. He looked at it and knew that it was perfect. He stepped inside and looked around. Then he climbed the staircase up to the roof and saw that his lookout would work wonderfully. He barked and howled to show how much he liked it.

*Call the Dog to the space. Let him check out his new house. As you narrate, he will look around and then climb the stairs to the roof. Let him bark and howl to show his approval. Once he is finished, the Dog can return to his seat.*

The next day the Architect was ready for anything. He figured that another animal was sure to walk in. But this time a Little Boy came into the office. He walked over to the Architect and said, "Could you build me a tree house please?" The Architect knew how to design one of these. He said he would do it. The Little Boy shook his hand and walked out of the office.

*Call the Architect to the space once more and let him sit down in his office. Then have the Little Boy enter the space and ask his question. They will shake hands and the Little Boy can return to his seat.*

The Architect got to work drawing pictures of what the tree house would look like. When he was done, he called his Builders once more. They looked at the cool pictures and got to work. They built and built and built until the tree house looked exactly like the one the Architect had drawn. When they finished, they went back home.

*Again, the Architect will sit down and draw. Call the Builders to the space again, have them look at the drawing and build, as they did previously. When they are done, they can all return to their seats.*

Soon the Little Boy came to see his new tree house. It was beautiful. He climbed the stairs up into the tree, opened the door of his tree house, and stepped inside. He knew that he would have many playdates and sleepovers in this tree house.

*Call the Little Boy to the space to look at his new tree house. As you narrate his inspection of the place, he will follow your instructions.*

That night, the Horse and her family lay down in their new stables, the Dog went to sleep in his new doghouse, and the Little Boy slept in his sleeping bag inside his new tree house.

*As you narrate, the Horse will come to the space and lie down. The Dog will do the same. The Little Boy (who may still be in the space) can lie down where he is.*

And as they all went to sleep, they thanked the Architect for making such beautiful new homes for them. The end.

Everyone stand up and take a big giant bow.

## FOLLOW-UP ACTIVITIES

**What Would Each Student Build?** In this story, the students learned how an architect designs buildings. The architect in the story just built homes, but architects also design big buildings. Discuss this with your students. Ask them to give you some examples of the different buildings an architect might design. You may want to give them some examples from your own town or city. For instance, the grocery store, the doctor's office, the Empire State building, or even a school can work as great examples for your students.

Call each student to the performing space and ask what kind of building the student would design if he or she was an architect. Let the child tell you about this building in as much detail as possible. This activity helps the students understand the parameters of an architect's job and encourages individuality and creativity.

**Cooperation.** To build buildings, architects do not work alone. They use cooperation. Talk about this with your students. If you have already used the cooperation lessons in this book, remind them that cooperation means working together. Ask them to tell you who works together to make these buildings and houses. Be sure to include the architect, his builders, and the painters.

Call all your students to the performing space to build a house together. Explain to them that they are going to work together to build a house of their own. This means that everyone has to help build it and paint it. Then let 'em loose to run through the space as they collect materials and build. Encourage the class to work on many different rooms such as the bedrooms, the bathrooms, the kitchen, and so on. When they have finished building, let them begin painting. As they paint, ask each child to tell the class what color he or she is painting the house. This activity will bring your class together and encourage cooperation.

**The Decorations.** Now that their house is built, the students need to add some decorations to it. Sit in a circle with your students and explain this to them. Describe the kinds of decorations that some people put in their houses. For example, furniture, pictures, and dolls are just some of the things that your students will get excited about.

Then go around the circle and ask each student which room of the new house he or she would like to decorate. Once the student has given his or her answer, let the child run through the space and decorate the imaginary room. Encourage each child to tell the class what he or she is putting in each room. This activity can also be done in pairs or even groups of three or four if you would like to keep the cooperation element of the lesson going a bit further.

# The Garden Story

## OBJECTIVES

- To teach students how plants grow

- To instill the idea of responsibility in students

- To have students consider the notion of long-term projects and commitments

## PRESTORY DISCUSSION

In this story, your students will be learning the intricacies of helping flowers and plants grow. Before you begin, take a moment to discuss what three things are needed to plant a garden: seeds, water, and sunlight. Some of your students may already be well versed on the ins and outs of gardening depending on your curriculum and their own experiences at home. If this is the case, ask the students who are familiar with the process to tell the class about their experiences. Otherwise, simply introduce the idea and the students will absorb the rest throughout the story.

## ROLES FOR STUDENTS TO CHOOSE FROM

| Role | Selling Point for the Students |
| --- | --- |
| Little Girl or Little Boy | Gets to dig and plant |
| Sun | Shines brightly on the garden |
| Water | Runs around and sprinkles the plants |
| Seeds | Slowly grows out of the ground |
| Mommy | Gets to act like a mommy |

As always, the role of the mother can easily be changed to a father if one of your students yearns to play a daddy. Also, the child in this story is written as a Little Girl, but can be changed to a Little Boy to suit your students' desires.

## STORY SYNOPSIS

A Little Girl decided to plant a garden. She went to the store and picked out some Flower Seeds. Then she went home and looked for the perfect place to plant them. She dug little holes, poured the Seeds in, and then covered them up. She watered them and knew that she had to wait for them to grow. The next morning she was very excited to see her flowers. But when she went outside to look at them, there was nothing there. After three days of this, she began to cry. Her

Mother came over to her and told her that it takes time for flowers to grow and that a gardener needs to be patient. So the Little Girl watered and waited. But, while she was waiting, the Sun was shining on the garden and helping the little seeds. Slowly the flowers started to grow. One day the Little Girl went down to see her garden and was overjoyed to see that her flowers had finally grown! Every year after that when spring started, the Little Girl would get some seeds and plant more flowers. And that's how the Little Girl came to have a garden of her own.

## NARRATOR

Once upon a time a Little Girl loved to play outside. She always looked at the trees and the flowers, and sometimes she wished that she could have some flowers of her own. So one day she said, "I have an idea. I will plant my own flowers." The Little Girl was very excited about this, and she set off to work right away.

> *Call the Little Girl to the performing space and let her skip around and look at the trees and flowers. Give her a moment to do this so that she can really begin to become part of the story. She will repeat her line after you narrate it.*

First she went to the garden store. She picked out some flower seeds and paid for them. Then the Little Girl took them home to her backyard.

> *Lead the Little Girl around the space as she walks to the garden store. As you narrate, let her look around the imaginary store as she picks out her seeds. You may even wish to ask her what color flowers she will be planting. You will act as the cashier and have the Little Girl pay you with imaginary money for the flower seeds. Once she's bought her flower seeds, lead your student around the room the opposite way to signify her return home.*

The Little Girl looked in her backyard for the perfect place to plant her garden. She really liked the tree where her tree house was, so she walked over to that spot to check it out. But when she got there, she realized that it was shady. The Sun didn't shine there. Her plants would never grow in the shade because they need Sun to grow. So she decided to look for another spot. She walked over to her swing-set. She looked around there, but she said, "No, people will step all over my flowers here." So she looked around some more. Finally, she found the perfect place: at the side of her house where there was lots of Sun and not too many people running around.

> *Point to where the tree house is and have your student walk over to that spot. She will check it out. As you narrate, make sure she shakes her head no to indicate that this spot is not good. Then point to where the swing-set is and have your student walk to that spot. She will check it out and then repeat her line after you. It will work best if the final planting spot is in the center of the space, facing the audience, so that they can see the actions that will follow.*

Now it was time to begin. The Little Girl took out her shovel and began to dig little holes. She dropped some Seeds into each hole. Then she covered up each hole. When she had used up all her Seeds, the Little Girl filled up her watering can and began to water the Seeds because flowers need Water to grow. Once the Seeds had been watered, the little girl wiped her hands and went back into her house. Now all she had to do was wait for the flowers to grow.

*As the Little Girl digs and fills the holes with Seeds, call the students who are playing the Seeds to the performing space. They will lie in the place where she is planting. It will work best if the Seeds curl up into little balls so that they will be able to grow up and out. As the Little Girl mimes watering the Seeds, call the students who are playing the Water to the space and let them dance around the Seeds. When she is finished watering, the Water can return to their seats.*

The next morning, the Little Girl was very excited when she woke up. She couldn't wait to see her new flowers. She ran downstairs and out the door, into her garden, and . . . there was nothing. No flowers bursting through the ground. Nothing. How could this be? she wondered. She thought that maybe she hadn't watered them enough. So she filled up her watering can again and watered them once more. When she was done, she went back inside and got ready for school.

*From where she is, the Little Girl can yawn to indicate that she has just woken up. You may have to do this with her for her to understand the transition. Have her run through the space and end up back at the Seeds. When the watering begins again, call the Water to the space and let them dance around the Seeds once more. Then she and the Water can return to their seats.*

The next morning, the Little Girl was very excited when she woke up. She was sure that her flowers would bloom now. She ran downstairs, out the door, and into her garden. But, again, there was nothing. Now the Little Girl was starting to get upset. Maybe her flowers would never grow. She sat down and cried. Just then her Mother came outside and said, "Why are you crying?" The little girl, who was very upset, said, "My flowers won't grow!" Her Mommy laughed and said, "You have to be patient. Flowers take days and days to grow." So the Little Girl had to wait.

*The Little Girl will hear her part again and reenter the space. As you narrate, she will sit down and pretend to cry. Some students find crying funny and others become embarrassed. Depending on your student, she may need you to put on the crying face with her. The Mommy will enter the space as you call her character. She and the Little Girl will repeat their dialogue. Be sure to break it up into enough small chunks that they will have an easy time remembering their lines. Then, the Mommy and the Little Girl can return to their seats.*

Every morning the Little Girl woke up and ran downstairs to see if her flowers had grown. When she saw that they hadn't, she watered them and went off to school. But, while she was at school, the Sun was shining on the seeds, and the seeds were growing little by little. And every day the Sun would shine a little bit more, and the seeds would grow a little bit more. Day after day, the Sun went on shining and the seeds went on growing and growing and growing.

*Once again, the Little Girl will run to the Seeds. As she waters them, make sure the Water comes into the space to do their dance around the Seeds. When she is finished watering the Seeds, the Water and the Little Girl can return to their seats. Then the Sun will enter the space. Let the Sun decide how he or she will shine down on the Seeds. Perhaps the Sun will stretch his or her arms out wide or repeatedly open and close his or her hands as though spraying rays of sunlight. As you narrate that the Seeds are growing, the students that are playing the Seeds can uncurl and gradually stand up as they grow bigger and bigger. By the end of this section, they should be full grown and standing tall.*

One day the Little Girl woke up, ran downstairs to her garden, and said, "Oh, boy! My flowers have grown!" She jumped up and down because she was so excited. Of course, she still had to water them and let the Sun shine on them so that they would continue to live. But now the Little Girl knew that she could make flowers grow.

*Call the Little Girl to the space and she will run to the full-grown flowers. Make sure she puts on her excited face as she repeats her line. Have her water them one more time and let the Water do their dance as the Sun shines his or her rays. Let them all continue in this vein as you narrate the conclusion to the story.*

And every year after that at the beginning of spring, the Little Girl would get some seeds and plant more flowers. And that's how the Little Girl came to have a garden of her own. The end.

Everyone stand up and take a big giant bow.

## FOLLOW-UP ACTIVITIES

Giving Flowers. In this story, the little girl grew beautiful flowers. What do the students think she will do with them? Pose this question to your students and see what kind of responses you receive. Some of your students will know that flowers are often given to loved ones or friends; others will not. Whatever the depth of their knowledge, make sure to let the students know that flowers are often given as gifts.

Call each student up to the performing space. Ask each child who he or she would give flowers to. Once the child has answered, give the child an imaginary bouquet and let him or her knock on a pretend door to deliver the flowers. This activity will get your students thinking about the people that they care about, and it will also teach them about the social functions of flowers.

Responsibilities. In this story, the little girl had a job that she had to do by herself — taking care of the flowers in her garden. When a person has something that he is in charge of, it's called a responsibility. Discuss this with your students. Remind them of the meaning of the word *responsibility* and have them repeat it a few times. Then have your students describe some of the responsibilities that the little girl in this story had as she took care of her garden.

Call each student up to the performing space one by one. Whisper a responsibility into the student's ear as he or she comes to the space, such as tying shoes, making beds, cleaning up toys, brushing teeth, getting dressed. Once you've given the student his or her responsibility, the child will act it out for the other students. The class will try to guess what responsibility the student is acting out.

Once everyone has had a turn, you may wish to sit in a circle with your students to take the activity one step further. Now that the class has become familiar with different kinds of responsibilities, ask each child to tell the class one responsibility that he or she has at home. Once everyone has had a turn, congratulate the class on having responsibilities. This will empower them and give them a sense of pride in the everyday things they do.

Plant Flowers. What kind of plant or flower would each student plant if he or she were planting a garden? Call the class to the performing space and have them all go through the same planting process as was told in the story. Let each student choose a spot in the room, dig, put in their seeds, and water them.

While everyone is waiting for the flowers to grow, go around the room and ask each student to tell the class what kind of flowers he or she planted. Most likely the children will identify their flowers by color only. The object is to remind your students of how plants are grown while letting them express a bit of their own individuality. Once everyone has had a turn, let the class pick their flowers!

# The Feeling Story

## OBJECTIVES

- To teach students about various feelings
- To help them to understand their own feelings and emotions

## PRESTORY DISCUSSION

Before you begin this story, take a few moments to talk to your students about feelings. If you regularly use the feeling warm-up, then your students will be familiar with the concept of some of the basic emotions. Take this time to remind them that a feeling is an emotion or a word that describes how a person is doing. Don't worry too much if they don't fully understand the concept by the end of your discussion. That's why the story exists.

## ROLES FOR STUDENTS TO CHOOSE FROM

| Role | Selling Point for the Students |
|------|-------------------------------|
| Little Girl or Little Boy | Gets to explore a secret forest |
| Grandma | Gets to act like a grandmother |
| Animals | Get to help the little boy or little girl |

In this story, your students can choose to be any animal that they wish. This is a chance to really let their imaginations run wild. The lesson plan has specific animals written into it for the sake of reader comprehension. However, feel free to change these characters based on student preferences.

## STORY SYNOPSIS

There was a Little Girl who didn't know what feelings were, so her Grandma decided to show her. She showed the Little Girl how to get to a secret forest by drawing a triangle and knocking on the wall of her closet three times. There, the Little Girl met a Horse and told him that she was scared. She met an Elephant who helped her to understand feeling angry. A Tiger taught her about being confused. The Little Girl met a Bird and knew what it was like to feel excited. A Chipmunk helped her to understand the feeling of sadness. And all the animals helped her to find her way home. Once she returned the Little Girl realized she had learned about many more feelings, and she thanked her Grandma for showing her the secret forest. And every now and then after that, the Little Girl would go into her closet and draw the triangle, knock three times, and enter the forest. She loved seeing all her new friends. And every time she went, she learned about more feelings.

## NARRATOR

Once upon a time a Little Girl lived in a house with her parents. One night they were having a party. The Little Girl was playing with some of her toys when her Grandma came in and said, "How are you feeling?" The Little Girl did not understand this question, so she said, "I don't know what a feeling is." The Grandma was very surprised. She tried to explain it, but it was hard. So her Grandma decided that it was time to teach the Little Girl what feelings are all about. She said, "Come with me."

*Call the Little Girl to the performing space and let her sit down to play with her imaginary toys. Then have the Grandma come to the space as well. The two children will repeat their dialogue after you.*

She led the Little Girl upstairs and into the Little Girl's own bedroom. She said, "I'm going to show you the Land of Feelings. Maybe you'll learn about feelings there." She opened the Little Girl's closet and pushed all the clothing to one side. She told the Little Girl to follow what she did. First, she drew a triangle on the back wall of the closet. So the Little Girl drew a triangle there too. Then, she made three circles, one in each corner of the triangle. The little girl did the same. Next, her Grandma knocked three times. And when the Little Girl did it, something very strange happened. The closet wall disappeared, and she was looking into a forest.

*As you narrate, the Little Girl will follow her Grandma through the space. You may need to lead them on this little walk. The Grandma will repeat her line after you. Then have them follow the instructions from the narration. Once the closet wall has disappeared, the Grandma can return to her seat.*

The Little Girl turned around to tell her Grandma how cool this was, but when she turned around, her Grandma was gone. Her closet was gone too! The Little Girl couldn't see anything that looked like her house or her room. All that was there was a strange forest. The Little Girl knew that she needed to find her way home. So she began to look around.

*Once the Grandma has returned to her seat, the Little Girl should turn around to look for her. To add additional amusement, you may want to encourage the Little Girl to turn in circles looking for her or to look in the corners of the room as though her Grandma might be hiding there. As you narrate, the Little Girl will walk through the space, trying to get home.*

Soon she met a Horse. The Horse galloped over to her and said, "Hi. How are you feeling?" The Little Girl magically understood what feelings were and she said, "I'm feeling scared. I'm afraid I won't get back home." The Horse said, "Don't worry. Just keep on walking that way and you'll get there." The Little Girl thanked the Horse and then watched him gallop away. She kept on walking in the direction that he had pointed.

*Call the Horse to the performing space and have him gallop over to the Little Girl. The students will repeat their dialogue after you. Then the Horse can return to his seat. Make sure the Little Girl puts on her scared face during this exchange. The Little Girl will continue to walk in the direction that she had been walking before.*

Next, she met an Elephant. The Elephant said, "Hi. How are you feeling?" This time, the Little Girl said, "I'm feeling angry. My Grandma should not have sent me here alone." The Elephant replied, "Don't worry. You'll get home just fine." The Little Girl thanked the Elephant and watched him stomp away. She kept on walking.

*Call the Elephant to the space and have him walk over to the Little Girl. The students will repeat their dialogue after you. Make sure that the Little Girl puts on her angry face as she says her lines. Then the Elephant can return to his seat and the Little Girl will continue walking.*

Next, she met a Tiger. The Tiger walked over to her and said, "Hi. How are you feeling?" This time, the Little Girl said, "I'm confused. I thought I was going the right way, but I'm not home yet." The Tiger said, "Don't worry. Just walk in three circles and you'll get there." The Little Girl thanked the Tiger, and the Tiger walked away. So the Little Girl walked in three circles, just as the Tiger had said.

*Call the Tiger to the space and have him walk over to the Little Girl. The students will repeat their dialogue after you and then the Tiger can return to his seat. Make sure the Little Girl puts on her confused face as she says her lines. Then have the Little Girl walk in three giant circles, just as the Tiger had instructed.*

Soon she met a bird. The Bird flew over to her and said, "Hi. How are you feeling?" This time, the Little Girl said, "I'm excited. I think I'm getting closer to home." The Bird said, "You are. Now just take three giant steps," and then he flew away. So, the Little Girl took three giant steps, just as the Bird had told her.

*Call the Bird to the space and have him fly over to the Little Girl. The students will repeat their dialogue. Be sure to have the Little Girl put on her excited face as she tells him that she is feeling excited. You may even want to encourage her to jump up and down to show her excitement. The Bird can return to his seat while the Little Girl takes three giant steps as she was instructed.*

Next, she met a Chipmunk. The Chipmunk said, "Hi. How are you feeling?" This time, the Little Girl said, "I'm sad to be leaving this beautiful forest." The Chipmunk said, "Don't worry.

You can come back anytime you want." Then he pointed to a tree. He told her to make the same symbol that she had made on her closet wall on the tree and she would find herself back home. She thanked the Chipmunk and he skittered away.

*Call the Chipmunk to the space and have him walk over the Little Girl. The students will repeat their dialogue. Make sure the Little Girl puts on her sad face as she says her lines. Then the Chipmunk will point to a different part of the room where the tree will be. He can return to his seat as you narrate it.*

So the Little Girl walked over to the tree. She drew the triangle with the three circles and then she knocked three times. All of a sudden, the Little Girl was back in her own room again. She looked behind her and the forest was gone.

*Have the Little Girl walk over to the spot that the Chipmunk had pointed to, as though she were going to the tree. Then she will make the symbols on the tree. When she learns that she is back in her bedroom, you may want to encourage the little girl to put on her happy or surprised face. You can do this with her to help her to understand the moment.*

Soon her Grandma came in and said, "So, how are you feeling now?" To this, the Little Girl said, "I'm happy to be home.

*Call the Grandma to the space once more and have the two children repeat their last lines of dialogue as the Little Girl puts on her happy face.*

And every now and then after that, the Little Girl would go into her closet and draw the triangle with the circles, knock three times, and enter the forest. She loved seeing all her new friends.

*As you narrate, the Little Girl will make the symbol one last time. Then call all the animals to the performing space and let them all run around and play with the Little Girl as they listen to the conclusion of the story.*

Every time she went, she learned about more feelings. And the Little Girl lived happily ever after. The end.

Everyone stand up and take a big giant bow.

# FOLLOW-UP ACTIVITIES

**Land of Feelings.** In this story, the Little Girl went to the Land of Feelings and told the animals how she was feeling. Let's take a trip there and see how the students are feeling. Discuss this with your students, and remind them of the Little Girl's journey in the story. Ask them to tell you some of the feelings that they learned about. Then ask the class if they know of any other feelings. Let them give you examples of some.

Call each child to the Land of Feelings by calling the class to the performing space one by one. Ask each child to tell you how he or she is feeling today. This activity is very similar to the one that is included in the warm-up section of this book. However, now that you have made feelings a bit more visceral for them, it will be interesting to see if their responses have changed or increased in depth or range. This activity is always great for helping your students to identify their emotions.

**The Feeling Charades.** Now that the students know all these new feelings, have them play a guessing game. Call each child to the space and whisper a feeling in his or her ear. Some feelings to use include: happy, sad, embarrassed, angry, shy, confused, silly, scared, and excited. Then have that student put on the face that goes with the feeling you have given them. The class will try to guess what feeling the child is showing.

Once each student has had a chance, sit in a circle and ask the class how it felt to make those faces. When they make an angry face, does it make them angry? There are no right or wrong answers in this circle. The point is to get your students talking about emotions and to help them identify these feelings.

**Feeling Match.** Have the students see how different things make them feel. Call your entire class to the performing space and let them spread out. In this activity, you are going to call out different situations, and your students are going to put on the face for the feeling that goes with them. For example, if you say, "Someone took your toy," your students might put on their angry faces. Some more things to try are: a birthday, a monster under the bed, losing a pencil, Grandma leaving to go home, spilling some juice. Feel free to add as many examples as you wish. This activity is a great way for your students to begin matching up the new feelings that they learned with experiences they have gone through. It will take the learning process one step further.

# The Story of the Seasons

## OBJECTIVE

- To teach students about the seasons

## PRESTORY DISCUSSION

Take a moment before beginning your story to refresh your students' memories about the seasons and what traits are typical to each of these time periods. Depending on what part of the country you live in, your students may know the seasons to different extremes. However, it's wonderful if you can help your students to understand not only what each season feels like in their part of the country but what it feels like in other parts as well. For instance, if you live in the South, perhaps your students are not as familiar with winter snowstorms as a class that lives in Chicago. But you are broadening their horizons by teaching them that wintertime in Chicago usually equals snow. Once you've touched on these new ideas with your students, you are ready to begin the story.

## ROLES FOR STUDENTS TO CHOOSE FROM

| Role | Selling Point for the Students |
|---|---|
| Mother Nature | Gets to act like a mommy |
| Fall | Gets to play in the leaves and pick apples |
| Winter | Gets to play in the snow |
| Spring | Picks flowers |
| Summer | Swims and plays at the beach |

## STORY SYNOPSIS

There was a woman named Mother Nature. Mother Nature was in charge of deciding the weather, and she changed it everyday to please each of her children. Their names were Fall, Winter, Spring, and Summer. One day the children were fighting over which kind of weather they liked best. Fall showed Mother Nature how much fun it is to play in the leaves and pick apples when the weather gets cooler. Winter showed her how much fun it is to build snowmen and drink hot chocolate when it gets cold. Spring showed Mother Nature how nice it is to pick flowers when it gets warm. And Summer splashed around in the ocean and built sand castles to show Mother Nature how nice it is when it gets hot. So Mother Nature told her children that they would all have to share. She split the year into four seasons and named each one after one of her children, making the weather of each season the way that it's namesake liked it best. The children were very pleased. And that is why the weather is always changing.

## NARRATOR

Once upon a time there was a woman named Mother Nature. Mother Nature was in charge of deciding the weather, and she changed it everyday to please each of her children. She could simply blow out a deep breath, and the weather would change. Mother Nature had four little children who were all very different. They were named Fall, Winter, Spring, and Summer, and they all liked different weather.

*Call Mother Nature to the performing space. As you narrate, she will blow out a deep breath to show how she changes the air. Then, as each name is called, have her children come to the performing space as well.*

One day the children were having a fight over which weather was the best. They were shouting and arguing when their mother came in. Mother Nature asked, "Why are you all fighting?" The children told her, "We all like different weather." Fall said, "I want you to make it cool all the time." Winter said, "I want you to make it really cold all the time." Spring said, "I want you to make it warm all the time." And Summer said, "I want you to make it really hot all the time." Mother Nature thought about it, but she couldn't make a decision. So she asked each child to show her why they liked these things so much.

*As you narrate the fighting, you may need to help your students get started. Once they have, let them argue for a moment. The students will then repeat their dialogue after you. Then have all the students return to their seats. (Another option is to have them sit on the floor in another part of the room to keep them involved in the story. However, beware that if you choose the second option, your students may not pay as close attention as when they are in their chairs in the watching space.)*

First, Mother Nature blew out a long breath and made it chilly for Fall. Fall ran around and had a wonderful time. He watched leaves falling off of trees and he raked up the leaves to jump in their piles. He went apple picking and picked many apples off of trees. He made apple pies and apple cider, and he shared these treats with his mother and his brothers and sisters. Mother Nature could see why Fall loved this weather so much and she invited him to come sit down with her.

*Have Mother Nature blow out a long breath. Then have Fall come to the performing space. He will watch the leaves falling and then pick up his imaginary rake. You may need to show him how a rake is used, as some children have never seen one before. As you narrate, he will reach up and pick apples. Once he has shared his apple cider with all the children, Fall can return to his seat.*

Next, it was Winter's turn. So Mother Nature blew out a long breath and made the air very cold. Winter loved it. He stood and watched the falling snow, and then he began to play in it. He made a snowman with arms and a face, and he even put a hat and scarf on the snowman. He lay down in the snow and made a snow angel. Then, he threw snowballs at his friends. When he was through, he had some hot chocolate to warm him up and went inside to sit by the fireplace. Mother Nature could see why Winter thought that this was so much fun. She invited him to come sit down next to her.

*Have Mother Nature blow out another long breath. Then Winter will come to the performing space, make a snowman, lie down to make a snow angel, and generally play with the snow. As he is drinking his hot chocolate, you may want to encourage him to blow on it to cool it down. It's a fun way to make the action a bit more real. Once he is finished with these activities, he can return to his seat.*

Next, it was Spring's turn. Mother Nature blew out a long breath and made the air feel a bit warmer. Spring loved this. She watched as the flowers began to come up from the ground. Then she ran through gardens and picked many, many flowers. There were green ones, red ones, orange ones, and purple ones. She gave bouquets of flowers to her mother and to her brothers and sisters. They all smelled the wonderful smells from the flowers, and they enjoyed them very much. Mother Nature could see why Spring liked this weather so much. She invited Spring to come sit down next to her.

*Have Mother Nature blow out another long breath. Then call Spring to the performing space. She will run around picking flowers as you narrate it. Instead of narrating the colors of the flowers, you may want to ask your student what color flowers she is picking. This will give her a chance to express herself in this role a bit more. Make sure that she gives a bouquet to each of the other students before she returns to her seat.*

Finally, it was Summer's turn. Mother Nature blew out a long breath and made the air nice and hot. This was Summer's favorite. She immediately put on her bathing suit and ran down to the beach. She jumped into the water and swam around. She swam under the water and met all the fish and then came back up again. Then she got out of the water, dried off, and decided to make a sand castle in the sand. She filled up her buckets with sand and dumped them out again and again. When she was done, she had the biggest sand castle anyone had ever seen. She finished her playtime with some lemonade, which she shared with her mother and brothers and sisters. Mother Nature could see why Summer liked this weather so much.

*Have Mother Nature blow out one more breath. Then call Summer to the performing space. She will follow your narration by jumping in the imaginary water and swimming around. She'll dry off and sit down in the sand to make her enormous sand castle. As she drinks her lemonade, make sure she shares with the rest of the children. Then she can return to her seat.*

Once all her children had had a turn, Mother Nature stood up and told them her decision. She said, "I see why you all like different things. They are all very special times. So we will share." Then she told her children that she would split the year into four times called seasons. Each season would be named after her children and would be just the way they liked it.

*Call Mother Nature to the performing space and have her repeat her lines after you. She's got a lot to say, so try to break it up into small chunks so that she is not forced to remember too much at one time. When she is finished, it's fun to encourage the rest of your students to let out a big, "Hooray!" to show how much they appreciate her decision.*

So every year during the fall, Fall gets to watch the leaves and pick apples. Every year during the winter, Winter gets to play in the snow. Every year during the spring, Spring gets to pick some flowers. And, every year during the summer, Summer gets to enjoy the hot weather by going to the beach.

*As you narrate this conclusion, let each student come to the performing space as his or her character is called. They will quickly reenact what you narrate.*

And that's why the seasons are always changing. The end.

Everyone stand up and take a big giant bow.

## FOLLOW-UP ACTIVITIES

### What's Each Student's Favorite Season?
In the story, the students learned how each season is different from the others. Go over these differences once more with your students. Now that they have been a part of this story, the traits of each season will be more accessible to them. Ask the class to name the four seasons. Then have them tell you something about each one.

Call each student up to the performing space. Ask that child to tell the class what his or her favorite season is and why. Then blow out a long breath and make it that season for your student. Let that child run around and enjoy the change for a moment. This activity is a great way to get your students thinking about their preferences while reminding them about what they have just learned.

### Planet Spin.
Is the story the students just heard a real story? Do seasons really change because of four children? Why does the weather really change? Pose these questions to your students. Most of them will know that the story is not real. For those who don't, gently explain that it was just a fun way to learn about the seasons.

Then discuss why the weather really changes. A good place to begin is with the sun. Ask your students to tell you what makes the weather hot, and they will almost always tell you that the sun does. Then follow this dialogue by asking them to figure out why it gets cold. Help your students to understand that when the sun doesn't shine as much, it gets cooler. Don't worry if they don't get it completely. The next activity will help them to understand it more fully.

Split your students into two groups: suns and planets. Place the suns in the center of the space and have your planets walk in a big circle around the sun. Tell your students that Earth travels around and around the sun. Then let them know that they are going to see how the sun makes Earth warm sometimes, and cold other times. First, have the planets walk forward and ask them to tell you which part of their body is getting the most sun (if they are walking counterclockwise, it should be their left side). That side should be the warmest. Then ask your students to walk sideways. Now their backs should be the warmest. Keep directing them to rotate and have the class continue to tell you what part of their body is the warmest. This activity will help your students to learn how the rotation of Earth affects the seasons. This process may be one that stops and starts. You can continue the activity a couple of times until your students really get the hang of it.

Once you have finished, it's always a good idea to sit in a circle and review what your students have just learned. It's a lot to take in, but your students will benefit from it.

# UNIT 7
# Creating Your Own Plays

Your students now understand how to tell a story in an organized and thoughtful fashion. They have learned about beginnings and endings and how to use their imaginations in ways that they may never have explored before. Now it is time to take this new knowledge and use if for personal expression. You will do this by creating your own plays with your students.

This section introduces you to two ways of letting your students create their own dramas. The Circle Stories are stories that you and your class will create together in a single class period, while the End-of-Year Plays are stories that will be rehearsed over a longer period of time with the goal of a final presentation. However, both activities are wonderful ways to bring your class together in the ultimate exercise in cooperation. They will be creating something together as a class, and that is an invaluable experience for children. The payoff will be golden.

In addition, working on the activities in this section teaches your students to work toward a goal. Whether that goal is presenting a play to their family and friends or simply creating a completed story together, your students will benefit from working on something that teaches them to think in the long term.

So have fun and enjoy the process of creating something new with your students!

# Circle Story

Now that you understand how to execute a drama lesson with your class, it's time to let the class create their own story to act out. You will do this by creating a circle story: a story that each of your students will have a part in writing.

## OBJECTIVES

- To let your students' imaginations travel to new places where the visions that they have can be expressed and realized

- To encourage your class to work together as a group to create something

- To empower students by giving them the freedom to shape a story

## ACTIVITY

Sit in a circle with your students. You will begin the story. Start off with the usual "Once upon a time," and then continue with the sentence and subject of your choice. Finish your opening with the words, "and then . . ." to prompt the student to your right to fill in the blank. Let that student continue, telling a new piece of the story. When you feel he has finished his section, gently stop him, look to the next child in the circle, and repeat "and then . . ." to prompt that child to begin her piece of the story. Go all the way around the circle until it comes back to you. You will then have the choice of wrapping the story up with a nice conclusion or letting the story continue for another loop around the circle.

## THINGS TO BE AWARE OF

Each student will have his or her own idea of how the entire story should go, and the child may try to get it all in during his or her turn. Try to be aware of the point at which the child's part of the story is finished, and if possible, end that child's turn at that point. Otherwise, you will have a very long story on your hands, and the children will begin to lose interest. If a student begins to ramble on (which will likely happen with many students), take a moment to stop the student and recap the most important points of his or her little diatribe. That way the class will not get confused, and everyone will be on the same page about where the story is going. Sometimes, the words *and then* are not enough to spark a student's imagination. If you find that is the case, it's just as easy to say, "and then what happened" to get the story moving.

You know your class dynamic better than anyone. If you begin to find that the students center their stories on fighting or egg each other on to use inappropriate words, you may need to make some rules regarding Circle Story. These stories should be fun for them to create, but the students should not feel like they have the freedom to use behavior and language that is normally discouraged.

## SOME GOOD STARTERS

Here is a list of some fun sentences to begin your Circle Story. However, you should always feel free to ask your students what they would like their Circle Story to be about so you can create your own opening sentence.

- Once upon a time, there was a little baby elephant and one day he turned pink.

- Once upon a time, there was a little boy who went to the zoo. He walked up to the giraffes, and then . . .

- Once upon a time, there was a bird's egg sitting in a bird's nest, and it cracked open. The baby bird peaked out, and said . . .

- Once upon a time, a lady looked out her window and saw a giant walking into the town. She ran outside and then . . .

- Once upon a time, there was a little fish that lived in the ocean. One day, he was swimming around and he got lost.

- Once upon a time, a little girl drank a flying potion. All of a sudden, she was lifted off the ground and then . . .

- Once upon a time, there was a big grizzly bear. He woke up one morning and started to roar, but he realized he had lost his growl.

## ACTING IT OUT

Once you have completed your circle story, it's time to make it come alive. Let the students choose which characters they would like to play just as you normally would. Then you will narrate the story that the entire class has just created while your students eagerly await their turn to be a part of the story.

Most likely this story will have many different twists and turns to it. You may feel the need to cut it down to its essence. The idea is for your students to see the story that they helped to shape. Not only will this empower them, but it will also teach them how to create and act out a story on their own.

# End-of-Year Plays

An End-of-Year Play is a wonderful way for your students to show what they have been learning in drama class, such as personal expression and memorization skills. In addition, it will give your students a sense of closure on the school year. The most important thing to remember when you are creating your play is to let it belong to your students. To this end, you will want to make sure that the children have a say as to what happens in the story. Of course, you can't hand over complete control to them; however, as you are rehearsing your play, consider each student's suggestions (which they are bound to have plenty of) and use the ones that you deem appropriate. You will find the result to be a more rich and endearing presentation.

## AUDIENCE

Before you even begin rehearsing your play, you will want to introduce the concept of an audience to your students. Undoubtedly, they have been aware that the other students are watching them when they are in the performing space during drama class. Now it's time to give the individuals in the watching space a title: the audience.

Once you have introduced the word *audience*, discuss the need to face the audience when they are performing. During drama class, it may have been OK for your students to face any which way, but now that they will be presenting something to an audience, encourage your students to face the audience as much as possible. As you begin to rehearse, you can encourage them even further. At first, just let your students know that an audience will be there to watch them and listen to them tell the story.

## THE INDIVIDUALS

In the two plays provided in this unit (*When I Grow Up* and *The Preschool Olympics*), the students play a large role in shaping the story. These are primarily adventure stories designed so that each child will get a moment in the spotlight. As the students begin working on the plays, you will want to ask each child about his or her specific role. For instance, in *When I Grow Up*, you need to find out what each of your students wants to be when they grow up. Or, in The *Preschool Olympics*, you'll need to know what activity each child thinks he or she does best. Try to ask your students these questions in private. This will prevent your students from copying one another's ideas. However, it's fine if it happens that two or more students choose the same thing.

Once your students have chosen their roles, they are ready to begin rehearsing. But beware: Your students, after making their first choice, will likely go through a period of constantly changing their minds. This is to be expected. Indulge them and let them try out different roles. They should have the freedom to create this play to their own satisfaction. However, let them know that one day they will have to make a final choice that cannot be changed. At a certain point, things must stop changing so that everyone can rehearse the play in its entirety. Be honest with your students about this, and they will respect your decision.

## REHEARSAL

You will probably want to spend about three to four weeks rehearsing your play. This does not mean that you need to rehearse it every day or even for an entire drama class during this period. The best way to get your students ready for the performance is to work in sections. Tell a little bit more of the story every time you rehearse, starting at the beginning each time so that the students are reminded of what they have already worked on. Then go over it again and choreograph anything that needs to be directed in a certain way. Once you've done this, move on to a totally different activity. You'll be amazed how much your students will retain.

During your rehearsal process you will assign lines to your students, much in the same way as when you teach a drama lesson in your class. The student will hear his or her name and then repeat the line after you. However, once you begin rehearsing and repeating the story over and over, the students will come to know their lines. Soon, all you will have to do is say each child's name, and he or she will say the correct line without your help.

## YOUR ROLE AS THE NARRATOR

As always, you will be playing the pivotal role of the Narrator. Your students have spent the year getting to know you in this capacity during the telling of a story, and there is no need to change that now. It's also a great way for you to guide the students if they forget what they are supposed to be doing. So have fun as you help your students to make a brand-new story!

# When I Grow Up

You will need to ask each student what he wants to be when he grows up. Their answers will help shape the play, and each child will have a chance to show what she will be doing in the future. To that end, in this chapter are nearly a dozen of the most common jobs students choose. You may find, of course, that one of your students chooses a job that is not presented here. By discussing with your student what the job entails, you can easily create your own scene for the student.

## I. INTRODUCTION

**All:** Ladies and gentlemen, boys and girls, presenting our . . . play! When I grow up, I want to be . . .

*One by one have the students announce loudly what they want to be when they grow up.*

## II. MAKING THE FUTURE MACHINE

**Narrator:** Once upon a time, there were some cool kids playing together at school, when all of a sudden _____ said . . .

**Student 1:** I have an idea. Let's go to the future.

**Narrator:** Everyone thought that this was a great idea and they all yelled . . .

**All:** Yeah!!!

**Narrator:** But, then _____ said . . .

**Student 2:** How will we get there?

**Narrator:** Everyone thought about it and scratched their heads until _____ said . . .

**Student 3:** Let's build a future machine.

**Narrator:** The kids thought this was a great idea and they all cheered . . .

**All:** Yeah!!!

**Narrator:** So they started to build. They built and built and built, until they had created an enormous machine that would take them to the future. When they were done, they all took three steps back to look at it, and they said . . .

**All:** Wow!

**Narrator:** But, _____ said . . .

**Student 4:** Hey, we forgot to paint it.

**Narrator:** So they began to paint. They painted it with beautiful colors. (Ask each child what color he or she is painting the future machine.) When they were done, they blew on the paint to dry it. Then they took three steps back and said . . .

**All:** Wow!

**Narrator:** And they all sat down inside their future machine. They put on their seat belts, turned the key, pressed all the buttons and counted to ten. Then . . . blast off! The children traveled five years into the future, ten years into the future, twenty years into the future! Suddenly they landed with a big kerplunk. And they slowly got out to look around.

## III. THE EXPLORATION

*As you tell this section, it will help you to have the students follow you in a sort of choo-choo train as you travel from place to place. Once they arrive at each destination, have them sit down to watch the student who is acting out his or her part.*

### The Spy

Narrator: _____ was a spy in the future, and he thought that he could help the kids figure out where they were. So he began looking for clues. He searched the area, hiding behind trees and using his binoculars. Finally he came back to tell the rest of the children what he had found.

*At this point, let the student who wants to be a spy tell the audience what he has found on his mission. It may have to do with the story, and it may not. Either way just let him have a chance to speak. If he has not helped the story along, you can conclude with this:*

Narrator: The spy also found out that they were twenty years into the future. So the children decided to explore some more.

### The Lion Tamer

Narrator: The children were walking along exploring when they met a ferocious lion. Everyone was scared, and they all ran to hide in a corner. Everyone except for _____. Luckily, he was a lion tamer in the future, and he knew just what to do. He took out his lion's whip and snapped it. The lion's roar got a little quieter, so the lion tamer snapped his whip again. The lion's roar got a little quieter, so the lion tamer snapped it again. This time, the lion started purring. The kids gave the lion tamer high-fives, and they all snuck past the purring lion.

*You can avoid a lot of the narration in this section if you play the roaring lion yourself.*

### The Artist

Narrator: Next, the children decided to go to a museum to see what art looked like in the future. When they walked in, they couldn't believe their eyes. _____'s paintings were hanging in the museum. She was an artist in the future, and her art was being shown in this museum.

*At this point, as the students are standing around looking at the paintings, ask the Artist what she painted a picture of. Let her take her time as she describes it in as much detail as possible.*

## The Baseball Player

Narrator: Soon the kids went to a baseball park. They were sitting down in their seats when they noticed that one of the teams playing was _____'s team. He was a baseball player in the future, and he was playing in this game. The game was tied in the bottom of the ninth inning and it was _____'s turn to bat. He swung at the first pitch. Strike one. He swung at the second pitch. Strike two. Then, when he swung at the third pitch, he hit the ball out of the park. Home run! _____'s team won the game! Everyone came over to pat him on the back and give him high-fives.

## The Dentist

*This part will take you out of the story a bit, but it's a fun way for the dentist to have a heroic scene. It will involve a bit of acting on your part.*

Narrator: Next, the children decided to . . . ouch. Wait a minute. Ow . . . oh no, it's my tooth again. Oh, I don't think that I can go on with the play. I've got a terrible toothache. Is there anyone who can help me? (The dentist will raise her hand and come on up.) You can? What will you do?

*Let the dentist tell the audience what she will do to your tooth to make it feel better (no matter how silly the answer is). Then let her perform her imaginary procedure and let the audience know how much better you feel.*

## The Ballerina

Narrator: Soon the kids went to a theater to see a ballet. They walked in and sat down in their seats. They were delighted to find out that _____ was performing in this ballet. She was a ballerina in the future and this was her company. The lights dimmed, the curtain went up, and _____ was on stage dancing. She danced a beautiful dance. And when she was done, the audience applauded to let her know what a great job she had done.

## The Doctor

Narrator: As they were walking along, all of a sudden, one of the children tripped over a rock and fell down. He hurt his leg pretty badly and wasn't sure if he would be able to keep on exploring with the other children. Thank goodness that _____ was a doctor in the future. He quickly ran over with his doctor's bag and fixed up that leg. His friend gave him a high-five for helping him out. Now the kids could go on.

*As with the dentist, you may want to take this opportunity to ask the doctor what he is doing to the student's leg to make it better.*

## The Policeman

*This section is also similar to the dentist's, as you will be stopping the story for a moment to do a bit of acting.*

Narrator: Soon the kids walked on and then . . . uh-oh. Oh no, I can't find my wallet. Kids, we can't continue with the play unless I have my wallet. I won't have my money or anything that I need. Can anyone help me? (The policeman will raise his hand and come over to you.) Oh, that's right. _____ is a policeman in the future. Maybe he can find my wallet.

*At this point, let the policeman search the space until he finds your imaginary wallet. The play will be saved and you can continue on your way.*

## The Fireman

Narrator: The children were ready to go home now, so they started back toward their future machine. But, when they got there, they had to duck down. The future machine was on fire. Luckily, _____ was a fireman in the future. He took out his hose and sprayed the fire until it was completely out. All the children gave him high-fives for saving them and the future machine.

## Superman

Narrator: The children were wondering how they would make their ship work now. They knew how to make it go into the future, but how would they make it go home? That's when _____ said . . .

Superman: I can do it!

Narrator: That's right. _____ was Superman in the future and he could definitely help them out. So the kids all got back into the future machine, buckled their seat belts, turned the key, and pressed all the buttons. Then Superman lifted the machine into the air and flew it back home. The kids flew five years back, ten years back, twenty years back.

# IV. ENDING

Narrator: When the kids returned, they were themselves again, not lion tamers, or spies, ballerinas, or firemen. They got dropped off at their homes, walked up to their rooms, and lied down to go to sleep. And that night when they slept, the children dreamt about what they were going to be like when they really did grow up.

The end. Everyone stand up and take a big giant bow.

# The Preschool Olympics

For this play, you will need to ask each student to tell you one thing that he or she is really good at. Some of your students will know that the Olympics involve sporting events and will tell you a kind of sport they are good at. Others will simply tell you about an everyday activity they excel in. Either answer is great. The idea is to create an entire play based around the things that your students feel to be their strengths. Once again, the following play gives examples of the most common "Olympic Events." If a student tells you he or she is good at something that is not in the play, you can easily create an event by having the student show you what the activity looks like.

## I. INTRODUCTION

All: Ladies and Gentlemen, boys and girls . . . presenting the Preschool Olympics.

Narrator: We'll show you what we're really good at, like . . .

*One by one have each student announce the activity that he or she will be doing in the play (or in the Preschool Olympics).*

## II. GETTING THERE

Narrator: Once upon a time, there were some really cool kids who were playing together, doing all the things that they do really well. All of sudden, _____ said . . .

Student 1: I have an idea. Let's go to the Olympics.

Narrator: Everyone thought that this was a great idea and they all yelled . . .

All: Yeah!!!

Narrator: But, _____ said . . .

Student 2: How will we get there?

Narrator: Everyone scratched their heads and thought about it. Finally, _____ said . . .

Student 3: Let's build a car.

Narrator: The other kids thought that this was a great idea and they all cheered . . .

All: Yeah!!!

Narrator: So the kids started to build. They grabbed pieces from all over and they built and built and built. When they were finished, they took three steps back: one, two, three. And they said . . .

All: Wow!

Narrator: But, _____ said . . .

Student 4: We forgot to paint it.

Narrator: So the kids started to paint it. They painted the car some beautiful colors. (*Ask each child to tell the audience what color he or she is painting the car.*) When they were finished, they took three steps back: one, two, three. And they said . . .

All: Wow!

Narrator: And they all got in. They put on their seat belts, turned the key, pressed all the buttons, and drove away. They drove around turns, up big hills and then down big hills, until finally they were at the Preschool Olympics. The children quickly got out of the car and went to sit on their team bench. It was time for the Preschool Olympics to begin.

## III. THE EVENTS

*It will be helpful if the students sit at the back of the space, watching their friends (facing the audience) during this section. That way they will still be a part of the play but will be sitting down to wait their turn. You can even give this seating area a name in your story, such as The Olympic Bench.*

## The Swimmer

Narrator: For our first event, we've got swimming. Will our swimmers please come to the Olympic Arena for the race. On your mark, get set, go. Look at him go. He's swimming across the pool with big strokes as fast as I've ever seen anyone swim. He's coming toward the finish line, and . . . he's a winner! Great job, swimmer.

## The Ice-Skater

Narrator: Our next event is ice skating. Let's watch as our skater glides around the ice. She's doing beautiful turns and big leaps. Here she goes with her big finale. Let's hear what the judges have to say about that. Judges . . .

All: A perfect 10!

Narrator: Great job. Congratulations, ice-skater.

## The Animal Petter

Narrator: Next up is our animal petter. He's very good at petting animals. Let's see how he does with this ferocious tiger.

*It will help if you act as the animal in this section. It adds a little humor and gives your student something real to work off of. All you have to do is sit down in the center of the space and roar like a tiger. The student will come over to pet you. Again, you can roar loudly. However, each time he pets you your roar can get a little softer until finally, you are purring.*

Narrator: Let's find out how he did. Judges . . .

All: A perfect 10!

## The Balance Beam Walker

Narrator: Our next event is the balance beam. Let's watch as the balance beam walker walks slowly across the balance beam. She's doing a great job. Look at those turns. Oh no, she's losing her balance. Good for her, she stayed on the balance beam. And now, she'll jump off . . . beautiful! Let's hear how the judges think she did. Judges . . .

All: A perfect 10!

## The Drawer

Narrator: And now it's time for our drawing event. Our drawer has been given a piece of paper, some paints, and some markers. (These should all be imaginary.) Let's see how he does. What have you drawn for us today? (Give him a moment to make his imaginary drawing and then have him tell you what he did.) Why don't you show it to everyone, and let's hear what the judges say. Judges . . .

All: A perfect 10!

## The Gymnast

Narrator: Here comes the gymnast for our next event. Let's watch as she tumbles and cartwheels. (If your student really is good at gymnastics, let her do a forward roll or a cartwheel. If she can't really do this, just let her roll herself around on the floor and do her idea of gymnastics.) Fantastic. Let's hear what they judges say. Judges . . .

All: A perfect 10!

## Numbers

Narrator: Our next event is in numbers. Today, our competitor will be writing a very difficult number: the number 3. Let's see if he's up to it. (If your student really is good at numbers, give him a real piece of paper with a marker and actually let him draw the number. Otherwise, it's perfectly fine to make this imaginary too.) Hold your number up for everyone to see. Looks great to me. Let's see what the judges have to say. Judges . . .

All: A perfect 10!

## The Runner

Narrator: Now it's time for our last race of the day. Runners take your mark, get set, go. Look how fast our runner is. I've never seen someone who can run so fast. Oh, look. They're getting close to the finish line. Here they come. And _____ wins it. Congratulations. Let's give him a hand.

## IV. ENDING

Narrator: It's time for our Olympians to receive their medals.

*At this point, it's really nice to call each student's name and have him or her step forward to receive his or her medal. You can easily make the medals in your art room by using paper and some ribbon. As you call each child forward, hang the medal around his or her neck and let each child receive a little applause from the audience.*

Narrator: And our Olympians lived happily ever after. The end.

Everyone stand up and take a big giant bow.

# THE END

You may have wondered, "How can drama be successful with such a young age group?" Now, you have the answer. By keeping your stories simple, active, and engaging, your students will thrive in a drama class and learn valuable lessons.

By using the lesson plans in this book, you have used drama both as a teaching tool and as a way to bring fun and excitement to the classroom. Stories and Fairy Tales introduced your students to storytelling and encouraged them to simply enter the performing space. Adventure Stories opened up the students' imaginations and helped them to explore new wonders. Moral Lessons will continue to teach your students right from wrong as they remember the characters and what each one learned in the stories. And New Ideas brought all these factors together to teach your students new concepts and ideas.

Having mastered the telling of a story with your students, you will feel more confident to create stories of your own. This will open a new door to your teaching and curriculum preparation, and make education more accessible to the students. Preschool students love to learn and now you have an exciting tool with which to teach them.

# About the Author

Nina Czitrom has gained her knowledge after more than eight years of teaching experience in New York City's public and private preschools. She currently heads the drama program at The Children's Garden Studio in Manhattan and has also served as a drama teacher at the Children's International Workshop, P.S. 3, Kids on the Move, and Oasis Children's Services. She holds a BFA from New York University's Tisch School of the Arts.